Learning to Breathe

• The story of twin micropreemies who defied the odds •

Heather Evans

Learning to Breathe

"Learning to Breathe" chronicles the author's experience with her children in the neonatal intensive care unit. All names have been changed to respect the privacy of the individuals.

Cover photo by Amy Kuntz and reproduced with permission from Amy Kuntz

Printed in the United States of America

ISBN-13: 978-1543072150
ISBN-10: 1543072151

For Hannah Grace and Gavin Michael

Prologue

When does one's story truly begin? Does it open abruptly when a tiny life bursts into the world, far too soon and gasping for just one lungful of precious air? Or does it begin earlier, warm and comfortable inside one's mother, nestled next to a sibling, oblivious to a hospital room conversation that has caused the world to come crashing down? Is it even earlier, during thousands of needle sticks because an embryo refuses to form, settle in, and grow? Or further back still, when two people meet and unexpectedly fall in love? We are an accumulation of all our moments, from the joyous celebrations to the crushing heart breaks, and as harrowing as our journey was, our life and our family would be remarkably different if even one moment had been changed. Therefore, we do not try to forget these memories, we do not push away the images in our heads of our children grasping at life, but instead we use them to learn, to teach, to appreciate, and to love to an even greater depth, one which I never knew existed before watching my two children balance perilously on the edge of life and death.

This is the story of Hannah Grace and Gavin Michael, miracles of modern medicine and the grace of God. This is the story of two children who took hundreds of prayers to be conceived and then thousands more to survive each day living in a world they should not have known for another four months. This is a story of strength conquering despair all because two one-pound babies continually refused to give up.

• Part 1 – Hope •

Chapter 1

2013

I WAS 21 WEEKS, 6 DAYS PREGNANT with twins and out of nowhere, I felt amazing. My husband, Brian, and I had struggled for four years with infertility, and we spent a great deal of the early pregnancy feeling cautiously optimistic. We had finally accepted that yes, I was in fact pregnant, I had made it past the first trimester and a half, and we were going to be parents after enduring years of loss. My early pregnancy had not been overly challenging, but like many expecting mothers, I had been nauseous with reflux and fatigue. Since the babies were conceived via IVF, Brian had plunged daily progesterone injections into my hip for the initial couple months to ensure the pregnancy continued. These, combined with the newly circulating hormones, led to panic attacks and mood swings. But that day, despite remaining a little nervous about having twins, I felt exceptionally good. Calm. It was a Friday and I was off work as I had already put in my four ten-hour shifts as a physical therapist. I had an appointment with my OB later in the day. Prior to pregnancy, I had spent years competing in marathons and triathlons, but carrying twins, I had decided walking was plenty of exercise. I stepped onto the treadmill in my basement that morning and strolled along, flipping through the pages of a magazine. I remember feeling more energized than I had in months.

Later that morning, I walked into the waiting room of my OB-GYN office. Through years of infertility, I sat in that waiting room for my annual appointments, feeling like I had been kicked, surrounded by glowing pregnant women, nervous-looking couples (newly pregnant, I was sure), and parenting magazines strewn about the tables. I felt a kinship with the older women who checked in, likely beyond the years of being pregnant. I wasn't the only non-pregnant patient after all. I dreaded the waiting room worse than the speculum exam.

Now, though, I was finally one of them. My belly had expanded enough that I had settled comfortably into maternity cargo pants. While I waited, I scrolled through websites on my phone, saving everything I thought I needed: how to make your own tutu, nursery themes, and first birthday smash cakes. I had finally reached the point where I believed this was actually going to happen, moving beyond the gut-wrenching experience of infertility. At our most recent sonogram a couple weeks earlier, we were told we were having a boy and a girl. We were thrilled to be blessed with a baby of each gender although we would have been equally happy with any combination.

As long as the babies are healthy, right?

I was called back for my sonogram. Warm gel was rubbed over my growing belly, and I watched the screen as the technician explained each area she was checking on both babies. Everything measured exactly as it should. Twins pose a higher risk for certain medical conditions, but there was no evidence of anything out of the ordinary. In fact, the babies posed perfectly, one lying on top of the other, so we could see silhouettes of both their tiny faces. The strip of photos scrolled out of the machine, and I tucked them into my purse, excited to show Brian their faces that night.

I saw my doctor who I knew very well due to my years of infertility. He had discovered the first problem four years earlier during surgery when he found a large dermoid cyst wrapped tightly around my right ovary, leading to the removal of the ovary, the fallopian tube, and a mess of adhesions that could only be explained by a previous cyst rupture. His name was Dr. Barrett and he had been an OB-GYN for over thirty-five years. He took measurements and checked internally, confirming all was fine.

Because of my complications getting pregnant and the fact that the babies were twins, Dr. Barrett has been cautious from the beginning. I was seen more frequently, every two weeks from the start of the pregnancy. On this day, he decided to order another ultrasound, this one an internal transvaginal ultrasound, to visualize the cervix in order to make sure everything was strong and closed as it should be at 21 weeks. I returned to the ultrasound tech, who this time helped me insert the transvaginal probe needed for the test. I had undergone this type of test countless times with our fertility treatments so I wasn't concerned, and I was already planning the errands I needed to run later that afternoon.

"I'm glad he ordered this. I see funneling."

I had no idea what she meant. I had medical training as a physical therapist, but I had never heard this term before.

"Let me run and get Dr. Barrett." She rushed out of the room before I could even process her comment and ask a question.

A sense of unease began to set in. This "funneling" was serious enough to warrant immediately tracking down a physician. Before I had time to grab my phone and start searching, she was back with my doctor.

He looked at the scan and confirmed the funneling. He explained this meant my cervix was dilating from the top (the opposite side from the dilatation that occurs with normal delivery) and this could lead to preterm labor. He was calm and reassuring, but wanted me on immediate bedrest, likely for the duration of the pregnancy. He also wanted me back in three days to rescan.

I left the office a little stunned, but at this point, his calm demeanor combined with my naivety on the issue led me to be primarily concerned with missing so much work. I ran the pelvic floor specialty program at our therapy clinic and I was the only therapist who saw these patients. I called Brian to relay as much as I had understood and, as I expected, he assured me all was most likely fine and I simply needed to rest. I called my office manager as I left the doctor's office and when I arrived home, I drafted a letter for him to fax to all the physicians I worked with explaining my program was on hold. My patients were contacted and informed their therapy was no longer available. The main feeling I had at this point was guilt in regard to abruptly cutting all of my patients off from their care.

After a quiet weekend at home on the couch, I returned to my doctor's office Monday. I continued to feel entirely normal which made being on bedrest seem nearly surreal. The recheck showed no worsening. My doctor explained the funneling would not improve so staying steady, as it had, was good. Everyone breathed a little easier and I went home to bedrest with another recheck in three days.

Brian had a birthday two days later. With me on bedrest, there would be no going out for dinner so I called in an order for us and he stopped by the restaurant on his way home from work, picking up his own birthday meal for takeout. Despite the funneling, I felt fine so we set up the meal in front of our TV and were able to relax the day before my next appointment. It's strange to look back now, picturing myself absorbed in a movie and take-out, while inside, my pregnancy was falling apart. It's amazing what a healthy dose of denial can do to you, especially when you feel the same as you did only a few days ago when everything was supposedly fine.

On Thursday, Brian and I went back to the doctor. Since the initial diagnosis, he had come to all of the appointments with me in case anything changed. With him there, I could breathe a little easier. His relaxed, confident approach to life directly opposes the stress that can sometimes consume me, creating the balance our relationship needs. When I start to worry, he keeps things light, making jokes and entertaining me and anyone we're working with including, at that moment, the ultrasound tech. He was the single reason I had survived the infertility nightmare. The tech began our ultrasound again and instantly, her light mood dissipated. Something was very, very wrong.

She rushed out with barely an explanation, returning with Dr. Barrett and a wheelchair. I stared at it thinking it couldn't possibly be for me; I felt fine. I knew they had to take precautions, but surely this was going to an unnecessary extreme.

Dr. Barrett explained the funneling had worsened. They whisked me into the wheelchair, quickly moving us to what looked like a procedure room. The tech told me not to push, and I remember looking at her like she was delirious. Why on earth would I push? They helped me onto a table and Dr. Barrett did a check, palpating my cervix, and for the first time since I had been told there was a problem, I felt sudden, searing pain.

"You're 100% effaced and dilated to a fingertip."

"What does that *mean*?"

I had heard the terms before, of course, but had not yet researched what they really even meant. Everything was happening so fast, and I couldn't process the information. I was only halfway through my baby prep book, and this was definitely going beyond how to manage reflux and sore breasts. I was supposed to have four more months to prepare.

"We need to get you across the street to the hospital. You could deliver tonight."

No.

This was not the way I lived my life. I planned. I kept my life organized. I never left home without my planner which was color-coded and highlighted. My babies could not simply come *four months* early. I had taken every prenatal vitamin. I never missed an appointment. I had done everything right.

Feeling blindsided, I stared at him and for the first time since they found the funneling, I began to feel truly afraid. I realized while on bedrest, I had been pushing away any negative thoughts, feeling certain that after all we had been through to conceive the twins, this could not turn into anything serious. Surely, we had suffered enough. I hadn't let myself fully contemplate the danger of the situation. I had imagined a lengthy bedrest, frequent doctor appointments, and likely preterm delivery - maybe 33 or 34 weeks instead of 35 which had been our goal with twins. But actual delivery – *now?* Could babies even survive this early? I was now 22 weeks, 5 days pregnant.

My official diagnosis was cervical insufficiency which meant my cervix had weakened too much to maintain the pregnancy. It was also referred to as incompetent cervix which left me drowning in both rage and shame. First, I had been incompetent at getting pregnant, and now I was incompetent to stay that way.

Two nurses were assigned the task of wheeling me to the hospital which was thankfully directly across the street. Brian walked beside us as they pushed me out into the sunshine and up the incline to the hulking building across the road. Dr. Barrett had given me some hope, saying he had delivered 22 weekers before who had survived. The quality of their lives was not further discussed, simply that they had lived.

They brought me to the antepartum unit, the wing where pregnant women were admitted, and I saw my initials being written on the whiteboard at the nurses' station. There was a sudden flurry of activity. Orders were received and insurance cards were taken. I was helped into a hospital gown and brought a commode to use as a toilet.

I was surprised by the commode. Could a ten-foot walk to the bathroom possibly bring on labor?

"At this size, the babies can just slip out. It's safer to get a baby out of a commode than a toilet."

I didn't ask any more questions.

Chapter 2

2007

BRIAN AND I MET AT THE GYM. I was in my mid-twenties, he was in his mid-thirties, and neither one of us were specifically looking for a relationship when we were introduced by mutual friends. He had a motorcycle, competed in triathlons, and was outgoing and unafraid to speak his mind, which both intrigued and rattled me. I was envious of his confidence and immediately drawn to him, if only as a friend at the time. I had run marathons for several years, and I had recently competed in a couple triathlons myself. I did fairly well at my first events, but there was a lot of room for improvement. I was still pretty clueless about many of the details so Brian took me under his wing and became my unofficial coach. He made adjustments to my bike, took me to a lake to practice my open water swimming, and helped me design a better training plan. We were both coming out of previous relationships and were not expecting anything beyond friendship and a training partner. I was at a point in my life when I needed a challenge, fresh goals, and a way to push myself beyond my comfort zone. Triathlons were the perfect outlet especially with a new, attractive friend guiding me through the basics.

I raced several more sprint races and fell completely in love with the sport. Typically, a person would progress from racing these shorter, sprint races to Olympic-distance (over two hours), to moderate-length distance, and then to long-distance triathlons. I was in so deep, however, that I skipped everything in between and signed up for my first long-distance triathlon which was 2.4 miles of swimming, 112 miles of biking, and a marathon (26.2 miles). These races in the United States fill up a year in advance so I had no options there. I didn't let it deter me and I chose one in France, recruiting one of my friends to travel with me. Looking back, it was not the most intelligent way to go about things, but at that point in my life, I was all about diving in without looking.

As I trained for France, Brian and I became closer and our relationship began to change. The training was grueling and could involve six or more hours on the bike in one day followed by an hour of running, often in heat over ninety degrees. Brian wasn't preparing for a race at this distance, but despite that, he began to give up all of his weekends to train with me. We spent every Saturday riding our bikes further and further as we explored all of the small towns around our city. Because of the volume of training, we also started to eat a *lot* and we began to fill our evenings trying out new restaurants or enjoying take-out while watching movies at his house. We fell into a comfortable routine, and I felt like I was spending all of my time with my best friend. Outside of work hours, we were rarely apart, sometimes zipping through the city on his motorcycle, other times swimming in pristine lakes as he showed me the best places to train. We were both enjoying being young and being outdoors, with limited responsibilities beyond the work day. Our friends began to think of us as a unit, knowing where one of us went, the other would be as well. We would stay up until the middle of the night chatting on the computer and when I would wake up groggy at 5:00 am the next day, it became obvious this was becoming more serious than either one of us had ever intended.

Two years later, after a hot yoga class, Brian asked me to marry him over fondue. After another six months, we stood aboard a sailboat at sunset, vowing to stay together in sickness and in health. At the time, we thought that meant our own.

Learning to Breathe

Chapter 3

BRIAN ARRANGED MY ITEMS in the cabinets of my hospital room, but I had planned a visit to the doctor, not an extended hospital stay, so all I had was my purse, shoes, and the last maternity outfit I would ever wear. So many people began taking turns coming into the room, it resembled a parade. Nurses arrived to check my vitals and place a belt around my abdomen to monitor the contractions I was in fact having without feeling them. Dr. Barrett came to make sure I got checked in, and he was followed by a social worker, a perinatologist, and representatives from the NICU upstairs. The NICU team consisted of a neonatologist and a neonatal nurse practitioner. They sat in chairs opposite my bed as Brian sat next to me, holding my hand. They handed me a yellow piece of paper that broke down a premature baby's statistics by weeks, by race, and by gender in terms of what percentage of babies lived and also what percentage lived without major disability. The statistics were startlingly grim. Before 23 weeks, baby boys had less than a 14% chance of survival and if they did live, only 7% lived without a profound disability. This meant a 97% chance of combined death or profound disability. The statistics were slightly better for girls than boys, with a 20% survival rate with 11% without profound disability, but all the information was brutally dismal. I couldn't stop staring at the paper. If I could just make it a couple days to 23 weeks, that would be just a little better. What exactly was considered a "major disability" anyway? I had some experience working with children with cerebral palsy as a physical therapist, but the range of disability was huge. Part of my mind focused on the fact that our twins just *couldn't* come now, not with these odds, while the other half tried to be brave, telling myself it didn't matter what happened, these kids were going to live and they would have every possible therapy they could ever need and then more. Brian tried to take the paper to keep me from obsessing over the odds, but I refused to let it go. The NICU team explained that should the twins come that night, at 22 weeks, they would not attempt intubation and life support unless the child seemed to be trying exceptionally hard to fight.

I had seen a perinatologist (otherwise known as a high-risk OB) following the initial funneling diagnosis, but by the time I had gotten to his office, there was nothing else he could do besides confirm the bedrest. Now that I was admitted, he was part of my care team, helping determine medications and tests. He sat down on the edge of my bed. There was nothing clinical he had to say that had not already been said. The odds were not good, but he was there for us. He held my hand as I sobbed and it seemed there were tears in his eyes. The unfairness and tragedy of the situation was affecting us all. These twins had to live; conceiving them took four years, four rounds of IVF, and an egg donor. There would not be another pregnancy. If there had been money left, which there wasn't, it would still not happen again; *these* were our children. I wanted these two only and there would be no more.

I was given a pill to stop the labor. I could only take it for a few days before it started to damage the babies' hearts. The steroid betamethasone was injected into my hip to speed up the development of the babies' lungs. I thought back to a prenatal visit I had very early in the pregnancy when Dr. Barrett had announced our goal was to deliver at 35 weeks. I had asked what develops last, what is most at risk with being five weeks premature and his answer had been "the lungs." If the lungs could be immature at 35 weeks, how developed could they possibly be at only 22?

The monitors miraculously began to show a slowing of the contractions. The babies' heartbeats were both stable. It was safe to say the babies were not coming that very instant as long as I remained monitored in bed so Brian ran home to feed our pets, gather work clothes for the next day in hopes everything had stabilized, and to retrieve all the items I requested – laptop, phone charger, deodorant, hairbrush. I was determined to have a lengthy antepartum stay. He arrived back and while we knew I was currently stable, I was also still greatly at risk to have the contractions return that night. We turned out the lights and Brian laid next to my bed on the plastic recliner. We decided together we wanted to choose names for the babies now. If the worst should happen, we wanted them to have perfect names, ones we had chosen when we had time to really think things through instead of ones assigned quickly in the midst of tragedy. Just one week before, we had started narrowing down a list of names I had collected over the several years of trying to get pregnant. Now, finally alone lying in the dark hospital room, we opened my laptop and ran through each name. We had not necessarily agreed with each other when tossing around names in the past, but two stood out to both of us that night. Brian pulled out his phone and we looked up meanings, added middle names, and quietly whispered the full combinations aloud to each other in the dark until we were certain we had the right fit for both children. The twins were named Gavin Michael and Hannah Grace. With the decision made, the nurse gave me the sleeping pill the doctor had prescribed and we both let go and drifted into sleep, knowing we had done all we could do. Whether the twins would arrive in the night was completely out of our hands.

Chapter 4

THE NEXT TIME I OPENED MY EYES, light was drifting into the room, soft slants sneaking in between the blinds. It was morning and the twins had stayed right where they belonged. They had been monitored throughout the night with no signs of distress. My contractions had stopped. The nurse came in with my medication, and I got another steroid shot to continue to hurry along lung development. Brian went to work which was thankfully close by, trying to save all possible vacation time for the twins' arrival. Both Dr. Barrett and the perinatologist checked in; the fact that I was still there and labor had slowed was monumental, but it was too risky for me to leave the hospital which was fine with me. I was terrified. I barely put weight on my legs when I transferred to the commode, afraid I would restart labor. I didn't want to sneeze or sit all the way up or even reach too far for my water. Brian and I talked nearly constantly throughout the day, and each time, I was able to tell him nothing had changed. One of the doctors told me, "Boring is good. We want boring."

We began to fall into an odd, hospital "home" routine. Brian slept on the plastic recliner each night. He would get up to shower for work in the morning and then he'd bring any toiletries I needed to my bed. He would cover the tray table with my dry shampoo, hairbrush, lip balm, and deodorant. He would bring me my toothbrush from the bathroom and a cup to spit. I no longer had any need for make-up, and I was too afraid of the movement it would take to change into clothes from my hospital gown. We would order breakfast and they would deliver it to our room. Brian would eat and head to work while I took my time as I didn't exactly have much else to do. The nurses were in and out to check my vitals and refill my water. Doctors would stop by to check in on how I was feeling. There was a brief discussion of inserting a pessary to hold the babies in place which is basically a support used for women who have pelvic organ prolapse. It was completely experimental in pregnancy with only a little published research in Europe, and the risk of actually triggering labor was too high so we declined and continued to simply wait it out. The doctors debated about placing a cerclage, stitches in the cervix to keep it closed, which Dr. Barrett had originally mentioned when he first found the funneling. It also posed a risk of triggering labor and research did not show great results with twins so we decided as a team that the risk outweighed the possible benefit. Instead, I remained flat and still. I read books and watched movies that friends had sent. I began doing some light arm exercises with the stretchy band the hospital physical therapist brought me, but I ignored all of the exercises that involved sitting up or moving my legs despite the doctor's permission.

A few days had passed and with each day, the babies' survival rate improved. At 23 weeks, the NICU brought me a new form. As they had explained the first night in the hospital, babies born under 23 weeks were not given life-saving procedures such as intubation unless the baby was making an extraordinary effort. At 23 weeks, however, it was the parents' decision whether the medical team would attempt intubation and life support. They would need our signatures if that was our choice.

Yes. *Please.*

My parents arrived at the hospital from Texas. They had been living there for six years and had wanted to return to Kansas City to be closer to us and the extended family. My dad had been watching some jobs, but when the babies began trying to push their way into the world more quickly than anticipated, the process accelerated. I reassured them I was fine for now and sent them forward on their house hunting. I desperately wanted them to move to the area and there was no reason to keep them in the hospital if they could go out and do something that might speed along their move.

Nine days later, I hit 24 weeks. It was Father's Day, and Brian had been scheduled to compete in a triathlon. I was stable so I told him to go ahead, but the stress level of the last week and a half combined with sleeping on a pull-out chair for nine nights did not lend itself to a good race so he passed. I examined my yellow handout from the NICU – at 24 weeks, the statistics improved to a 58% chance of survival and a 40% chance of survival without a profound impairment. The odds were still staggering, but they were significantly better than they had been before. As everyone kept repeating to us, every single day gave our babies a better chance at life. One additional day of lung development could make a life-changing difference.

For the first time since I was admitted, a nurse brought in a scale. I stood on it and was told I had lost three pounds since my first day in the hospital. Had I gotten close to 35 weeks, they had expected I would gain about 45-50 pounds. At this point, I had only gained 17. When the doctors were informed, they jokingly told me to eat more pie, but I took everything seriously at this point so I began adding slices to every meal.

I remained restricted to the commode, but for the first time, I was allowed one walk with a nurse to the bathroom to take a shower seated on a chair. After nine days without a shower, I ignored any remaining modesty and let the nurse strip away my hospital gown and situate me on the seat. Brian stayed to hand me soap and shampoo, and I enjoyed what was undoubtedly the best shower of my life.

That afternoon, Dr. Barrett came in to tell me he was going on vacation for about a week. He patted me on the leg.

"I want to see you right here when I get back."

Some friends came to visit that night, friends we had not seen for a while but genuinely good people you can always count on to show up for you when times are challenging. It had been a great day with only one small red flag. I had noticed a small puddle on my sheet when I got up earlier in the day. The nurses used a test strip to see if it was a leak of amniotic fluid. The reading was negative, but they would inform the doctors.

Brian and I settled in to go to sleep, used to our routine now, knowing he had to go to work the next day as it would be Monday morning. Shift change for the nurses was at 7 pm. My day nurse told my night nurse, "This is the easiest patient you'll ever have."

Chapter 5

2007

MY FRIEND, KATIE, AND I ARRIVED in Nice, France a few days before my triathlon after I had trained for six months. The postal service had lost my newly issued passport and it arrived just two days before our flight. When we landed in France, we learned the airline had lost my bike. Out of seven hundred or so participants, under a hundred were women, most did not speak English, and at 5 foot 2 and under 100 pounds, I was smaller than almost everyone. All of these could have been interpreted as signs I should not be attempting this race, but I ignored any type of superstition and just dealt with one issue at a time. The night before the race, my bike was shipped to our hotel from where it had been lost in Heathrow and I shed tears of relief (as did the lovely somewhat-English speaking couple who owned our hotel who had been trying without luck to help me, I'm sure). Race morning arrived, and everyone in our hotel was up around 3:00 am. After a quick breakfast, Katie and I set out on foot toward the start of the race with me suited up in a jacket and a pair of Brian's old sweatpants over my race gear. As hundreds of us donned our wetsuits and marched down the rocky beach to the start, the helicopters circled overhead and jet skis zipped back and forth across the Mediterranean Sea. The intensity of the moment brought tears to my eyes; after focusing on training for six months, this was the day it all happened.

The sound of a horn pierced the morning. My race had officially begun.

The swim was two large circles in the Mediterranean Sea totaling 2.4 miles. The water had been cold and choppy during practice the day before, but it had calmed by race morning. I had done plenty of open water swim practice, but nothing that could prepare me for swimming with hundreds of other seal-like, wetsuit-clad participants less than an inch away. The benefit of swimming with that many people, though, was that the draft picked you up and whisked you along as you swam. I was out of the water after my first loop in less time than I had predicted. On the second loop, the swimmers had gapped out more, there was no draft, and it was tougher, but it was still very manageable and next thing I knew, I was out on the beach running into the changing tent, racing past Katie who was rattling a cowbell and yelling my name.

The bike course was 112 miles in the Alps. Perhaps I hadn't thought this entirely through when I picked this particular race. My background was as a runner, not a cyclist. I quickly began to notice that most racers were on road bikes made for climbing, as opposed to my more aggressive tri bike, and also most participants were, well, European men. I pedaled along after the men noting the names on their race bibs- "Franz, Juan, Sebastian." I went up and up and up the mountains. The scenery was breathtaking as I looked over cliffs sprinkled with homes and apartments surrounded by lush greenery, overlooking the turquoise sea and rock beach below. I had plenty of time to take it in because of the fact that I was grinding away slower than I had ever trained as the incline on the mountain never seemed to stop. Occasionally, I would ride through a small town and a few people would dot the side of the road, cheering in French. Then I would be alone again, pedaling for another eternity. At some point, I reached the top and turned back down the mountain however I soon realized I would not be making up any time as I had hoped. The roads were steep, sharp, and curved. My bike skills were not good enough to race down that type of terrain in my aerobars like the professionals and every time I saw a cyclist lying on the side of the road, bloody, and trying to unclip from their pedals, I would further accept my reduced speed. It took seven and a half hours for me to cover the 112 miles on my bike, well over an hour more than I predicted, enough that Katie was concerned down below. I could barely sit on my saddle any longer, I was so sore. As I handed my bike off to the volunteer at transition, I probably would have sold it to him I was so finished.

Yet there was still a marathon. After a decent swim and a brutal bike, we were now at the start of running 26.2 miles. I had completed over ten marathons at this point, including Boston just two months before, but never after working out for nearly nine hours. I set out on my mission to complete four loops that were a little over six miles each. I tried to hold my pace as steady as possible knowing it was only going to get harder as I got to the final loops. Brian and I had trained intensely on nutrition and I had always done well in marathons taking in water and chocolate energy gel, but at this point, I was so nauseous I couldn't choke it down. For over four hours, I jogged through the sun along the Promenade de Anglais, stopping occasionally for sips of soda and bites of crackers, the only two things my stomach wouldn't reject. I realized I had been racing for almost an entire day. The spectators cheered and Katie faithfully rang her cowbell every time I passed her. Light glinted off the ocean and I could barely believe I had come so far in my first long-distance triathlon, but I was starting to get very, very tired. Part of me began to question the point in the whole endeavor while another part of me was brimming with excitement for being so close to the completion of such a monumental goal.

The skies turned to dusk as I finally hit the last lap of the run. Participants around me were walking, no longer smiling. Some were sitting on the curb, looking defeated. Volunteers swept the road which was littered with empty water cups and energy gel wrappers. I kept running. It wasn't fast and I took short walk breaks, but I continued to simply shuffle one foot in front of the other. A few miles from the finish, it was almost desolate. Lonely. It was dark, there were few spectators, and no one would have noticed if I stopped or left the course to take a walk to the beach instead. As badly as it hurt, though, I forced myself to push through toward the end. As I came closer to the finish, more people lined the roads and the darkness began to fade away. I could see the finisher chute with spectators standing five deep on both sides. There was music, something techno in French I couldn't understand but suddenly loved. My pace picked up, renewed after thirteen hours of racing. I ran toward the bright spotlights ahead, illuminating the racers as they finished their day. Other racers who were a lap behind had to simply turn away from the celebration to head out for yet another loop into the dark. I surged up the ramp to the finish line with my arms held weakly above my head. I had done it. I had battled the training, the obstacles, and the Alps, and I had finished my first long-distance triathlon in the French mountains, of all places.

Afterward, Katie sat by me, relaying me with stories of the day's excitement as I lay flat on my back on the pavement with participants walking all around me. Little did I know, Brian was at home, painting the back of his SUV window with proclamations of my accomplishment. Life had hit a peak, and I could never imagine pushing through something so grueling again. In actuality, it was only a small preparation, one that would help give me strength to make it through the rough road six years in our future, on the fourth floor, in neonatal intensive care.

Chapter 6

I WOKE UP TO A WAVE OF PAIN. It wasn't terrible, similar to a strong menstrual cramp, and it took a couple of minutes before I fully opened my eyes and realized something was wrong. I woke Brian, and we pressed the call button for the nurse. I shifted onto the commode and saw blood, not much but enough to know something in my status had changed and it was not good. Brian switched on a dim light, and I saw it was 1:25 am. Somehow, seeing the time made me realize the seriousness of the situation. It wasn't 6:00 am as I had hoped; I definitely had no explainable reason to wake up at 1:25 in the morning unless something was wrong.

My nurse strapped monitors around my belly and confirmed everyone's suspicions: contractions. She paged the on-call OB-GYN who was someone I'd never met. I had been so attached to Dr. Barrett, I had never even scheduled an appointment with anyone else. He told me all along that as long as he was in town, he would deliver the twins whether he was on-call or not and he would only be gone one week of my pregnancy, right around 24 weeks. At the time, I had blown that off; 24 weeks, that would leave us plenty of time to spare.

The new doctor wasted no time. She checked and announced I had started to dilate further. She wanted catheter placement and an IV. Magnesium sulfate was ordered to try to stop the preterm labor and also to protect the babies' brains from severe cerebral palsy. I was 24 weeks, 1 day pregnant.

Once the magnesium sulfate began to drip through the IV and enter my bloodstream, I was enveloped in nausea. Within seconds, I felt like I had contracted a terrible flu on top of the contractions which continued every few minutes. My body was on fire. The nurse dropped the temperature in my room and everyone quietly added sweatshirts while I sprawled on the bed with the soaked sheets stripped away and a cold washcloth draped across my forehead. The lights were raised to full intensity, and a catheter was inserted which was a knife-like pain much greater than the contractions. It was decided that I would be transferred to labor and delivery, down the hall from antepartum, in case labor could not be stopped. We piled as many of my belongings as we could on my bed which the nurses wheeled down the hall while Brian made multiple trips back and forth carrying laptops, wheeling a cart of flowers, and all the while, calling our parents. When we reached labor and delivery, I had a new nurse and she opened up small shelves from the wall which I learned were warming tables. The babies were still so small and premature that a controlled c-section environment would be much preferable to a sudden vaginal birth, but the warming tables were ready in case they suddenly slipped out. *Slipped out.*

The shift had changed, and a new OB-GYN arrived to check me and announced I had continued to dilate. She would check on another couple patients and return again. A neonatologist from the NICU came down to emphasize how vital it was for babies born this early to receive breast milk and also to ask for their names.

"We like to start talking to them right away, and we like to call them by their names."

Even now, I don't know if medication other than magnesium sulfate had been given, but somehow the pain from both the catheter and the contractions had melted away. It was a deceiving effect, though, because while I felt like everything had return to normal, the monitors draping my belly and the doctor who returned to recheck assured me this was not at all the case. The contractions were frequent, despite the fact that I couldn't feel them, and I continued to dilate. At 11:30 in the morning, she examined me, peeled back her gloves, and announced it was time to move to the operating room for the c-section. She told one nurse to call the NICU (I later learned a team in the NICU had already been on stand-by, waiting), and another nurse instantly appeared with a gown and head covering for Brian.

As I was wheeled into the operating room, I was shocked at how intensely bright it was with large overhead lights reflecting off the hulking pieces of metallic equipment. The room seemed enormous, and it was already a flurry of people in scrubs moving quickly as everyone performed their individual tasks. At the time, I had no way to know that people were also rushing about, one level up in the NICU. Months later, I would be there when a set of 24 week triplets were about to be born. Curtains in NICU rooms were quickly pulled tight, but you could hear footsteps running down the hallways and hurried voices going over last minute instructions and details. Then, just as quickly as the sounds had started, there was silence as the teams had gone down to the delivery of the triplets and everyone, including the NICU parents, held their breath, said silent prayers and waited.

At first, Brian was not allowed in the operating room while I was prepped for surgery. I already had an IV and a catheter so we moved directly to me sitting on the edge of the table while a needle was plunged into my lower back. I transferred to another table and my legs were bent when the block took effect which meant a few seconds later, I looked down and was completely bewildered to see my legs were in fact straight. I was laid back, my arms were secured out to the side, and a blue sterile drape was lifted at my chest. Brian was suddenly by my side holding one of my hands and a nurse anesthetist was seated by my other shoulder. Two surgeons arrived, preparing to begin, and what I could not see beyond the drape were the two NICU teams scrubbed in, waiting for their tiny patients to be delivered. There were two tables ready and around each one stood a neonatologist, a neonatal nurse practitioner, a nurse, and a respiratory therapist, ready to attempt miracles.

Things began to get a little hazy. I was suddenly overcome with nausea and tried to signal Brian to tell the nurse as I turned my head and began to throw up. My blood pressure had dropped very quickly and my medication was adjusted. I began to feel strong tugs on my stomach. I knew the incision had been made.

Gavin was transverse, lying sideways instead of head down. The doctor informed me this would require her to make the incision in my uterus in such a way that any future deliveries would require a c-section without question. It really meant nothing to me; I still had such faith these children would live and I did not care in the least what they did to me in order to save them.

Hannah came first. They lifted her above the drape for a few seconds; she was so small, too small, eyes fused shut, and she was blowing bubbles. I could only see her for a couple seconds because, as expected, she was unable to breathe on her own. She was whisked to her NICU team for immediate intubation. I found out later that she tried to give a small cry, miraculous for a baby with such immature lungs.

Gavin came next, but not as quickly. Being transverse, it took more maneuvering to get him out, but then there he was, above the drape for a second, before being rushed away. I couldn't see anything as I was lying flat while my surgery was completed, but Brian could see the NICU teams and he told me, "They're still working on Gavin." As predicted, being a little boy, Gavin's lungs were even less developed than Hannah's, making him even sicker. Later, I learned it took multiple attempts to intubate him; his heart rate never stopped all together but it dropped dangerously low, and the team had to perform chest compressions to aid his tiny heart while intubating his failing lungs.

My mind flashed to photographs of friends after a c-section with a chubby newborn baby held above the drape next to a mother's smiling face, with a grinning, scrub-clad father leaning his head in close to the child. Surgery, but happy and safe. Mother and baby doing well.

This c-section was not like that.

While Gavin's team continued to work in the operating room, Hannah's team had stabilized her enough to hastily push her bed up to the NICU. They stopped for just a second by my head so I could try to see her. Her nurse smiled.

"Congratulations, Mom."

Everything stopped, if only for a second. Since 1:25 that morning, this had been a medical emergency. This day had been about sudden surgery, crippling fear, beating odds, and miraculous medical undertakings. When Hannah's nurse spoke those words, it reminded me that amidst all of the urgency, delicacy, monitors, and fear, this was still the birth of children. Whatever happened next, two children had been born; yes, too early and yes, undeniably and dangerously sick, but they were now officially a part of this world on the outside. For the first time, I was a mother. There would be no teary photographs of parents cradling a baby minutes after birth, no rolling out of the hospital in a wheelchair a few days later with a baby bundle in my arms and balloons fluttering above my head, but I was a mother nonetheless. I will never forget that moment and how her words transformed it all.

Several minutes passed and Gavin's team was still working. The surgeons were closing my c-section so I continued to lay flat with my arms pinned straight out, unable to see or hear what was happening.

Out of nowhere, they were moving. They couldn't stop by my bed the way they had with Hannah because Gavin was fighting so hard to breathe. If Hannah's team had been pushing her quickly out of the room, Gavin's team was sprinting. Someone told Brian he could go with them, and he looked down at me on the table.

"Go! Go!"

Brian was gone, both babies were gone, the NICU team of eight was gone, and suddenly, everything seemed strangely quiet. For the OB-GYNs, the emergency was over and, other than the quiet, I remember nothing from this point. Somehow, my surgery was completed and I was wheeled back to labor and delivery, but it's all black whether from medication or from being completely overwhelmed by it all. What I remember next was being allowed very careful ice chips while a nurse performed a painful massage-like procedure directly on my abdomen every few minutes, and this apparently snapped me back to reality. Then, Brian was back.

Despite the fragility of the situation and the illness of the twins, he walked in smiling the proud smile of a new father and handed me his phone on which he had thankfully taken pictures. Both babies were impossibly small with their eyes fused shut, swimming in pink and blue hats which had been folded over multiple times. Gavin's face was bruised to a purplish color because of his position inside me and the way in which he had to be removed. Hannah was reaching out the smallest hand, no larger than a fingernail. They were wrapped in what looked like clear plastic bags with ventilator tubes down their throats and wires protruding at every possible angle.

Brian had statistics; this time, heights and weights not odds of life and death. Gavin was 1 pound 9 ounces and 12 inches long. Hannah was 1 pound 8.5 ounces and 11 ¾ inches. He began to text out the photos and make calls to our parents followed by our close friends. I listened as much as I could, but then the nurse would come back to knead my abdomen again and it was hard to hear or see anything while she was doing that.

Most people have heard of premature infants being referred to as preemies. I even had a doll as a child who was a "preemie." She looked just like the other adorable baby dolls, but she just happened to be a little smaller. What most people don't know is that there is an additional designation for the smallest of these preemies. Those born before 26 weeks or under two pounds are referred to as micropreemies, a term which almost sounds cute but in reality represents babies who are dangerously sick, unable to breathe, and straddling the border of life and death on the edge of viability. These are not the babies that inspire dolls given to young children. Gavin and Hannah, born at 24 weeks 1 day, were easily assigned micropreemie status.

Another blank space in the memory, and then we were moving to the mother/baby unit only in our case, no babies. A team of nurses took us upstairs to the NICU first and since I had to lay flat for twelve hours, this meant they took me and my entire bed. My drug-induced memories are hazy and incomplete. I've tried desperately to recall seeing my babies in their rooms for the first time, but maybe in reality, it's good that my brain stored the images of my children struggling for life in a location I can't access.

We spent the afternoon in mother/baby. At some point, I'm sure we must have slept and ate, but my memory is cloudy. I think some friends came to visit, and I had conversations I don't remember. Pain medication led me to fade in and out between fear and fitful sleep. Brian went back and forth to the NICU, bringing me updates. Day turned to night and near midnight, twelve hours after my surgery, a nurse came in to help me sit up on the edge of the bed for the first time to try to pump breast milk. The abdominal pain in sitting was excruciating, and I didn't manage even a drop of milk. It was too early; my body was confused and had no idea that it was time to produce milk. My nurse assured me this was normal and helped me lay back down in bed.

About an hour and a half later, I was gently wakened again. I had known the midnight wake-up call to pump was coming, but this was unexpected and, therefore, immediately alarming. A woman sat down next to my bed and introduced herself as one of the neonatal nurse practitioners from the NICU.

"I just wanted to come let you know that Gavin is not having a very good night."

My heart seemed to momentarily fail. They had sent someone down from the NICU in the middle of the night to tell me my son was not doing well. I could barely ask the question.

"Is he...could he...is he in danger of...?"

"No, no. He's just very sick. We wanted to tell you we had to move him to a higher level of ventilator called an oscillator and we've given him two doses of surfactant to help his lungs. He's more stable now."

After she left, I felt completely lost as to what to do. My child was struggling despite being on life support, and I was trapped a floor below in bed after surgery, unable to rush to his side. Brian and I were trying to figure out what to do next when my night nurse appeared in the doorway, lit softly by the moonlight.

"Would you like to go see him?"

I hadn't known this was even a remote possibility, and I didn't want to dwell on why they might be making this exception.

I desperately wanted to go upstairs even though I was terrified. She looked toward a wheelchair that I only now noticed was in my room and made a move to retrieve it for me. With no time to waste, though, I snatched up my catheter bag, stepped out of bed, and walked across the room to the chair. Just ninety minutes earlier, I would have described pain with simply sitting in bed as excruciating yet I felt no pain at all as I walked across the room. I had to get to my babies.

I was wheeled upstairs and this time, despite it being the middle of the night, the drugs were wearing off and I could really take in the NICU. After scrubbing in at the sanitizing station, we took an immediate left down the first row. There were four babies on each side. I would later learn this was not the row for the fairly healthy babies they called "feeders and growers," this row was for the most critical babies. This was home for the smallest of the preemies. Hannah was in room 3 and Gavin was in room 4, and they had a sliding glass door between them. I asked the nurse to park me at Hannah's room first.

I picked up the catheter bag and padded, barefoot, to my daughter. The lights were dimmed and there was only moonlight from beyond the windows however the monitors cast an eerie greenish glow into the room. Being born so early, the babies could not regulate body temperature so they were both in fully enclosed glass containers, called isolettes, with two portholes on each side. These isolettes not only maintained temperature, they also added humidity so the twins were basically basking in what felt like a tropical rainforest. Since they were so premature, each of the twins had a nurse constantly at the bedside. Hannah's nurse was warm and friendly; she waved me closer so she could explain the tubes and wires running all over and around our beautiful, if tiny, baby girl. The tube down her throat went to her lungs and attached to the ventilator ("vent," as we would come to call it), another wire ran to the pulse oximeter on her foot constantly measuring her oxygen saturation level, another to an IV, another to a temperature probe. Two lines emerged from the umbilical area where she should have still been attached to me for another four months, one going into an artery that could monitor her blood pressure and another into a vein that gave access for fluids and medication. Hannah was sick, but stable. Her nurse showed me a bulletin board in her room that was empty except for a timeline of goals for each week. I could feel free to decorate the rest of the board. I tried to smile at the nurse while I attempted to absorb all of the information, but it seemed too surreal. These couldn't be my babies, the ones who had been inside me, beneath my skin and listening to my heartbeat, only fourteen hours before. Hannah looked like a doll. A very, very small doll. She didn't move at all. I stood at her isolette watching the ventilator provide breath after breath, trying to push from my mind the fact that this tiny baby, who was only alive because of the vent, was my healthier baby.

She looked like a baby bird, fallen from her nest.

I made my way to Gavin's room and was immediately struck by all of the noise. His nurse flashed a quick smile, but was obviously under more stress with him. Being on the oscillator versus the regular ventilator was the cause of all the sound. I began to make my way through the maze of massive gray machines, glancing cautiously at their knobs, dials, and screens. Tubes and wires cascaded down, attached on one end to a machine and on the other to an impossibly small baby enclosed in glass.

Gavin was just as small as his sister with purplish bruising on his face and a yellow disc positioned over the side of his head. The nurse explained this was his "earmuff," covering his exposed ear, because of the intensity of sound coming from the oscillator. While Hannah's ventilator made hissing sounds at regular intervals, in turn leading to chest expansion at those times, the oscillator ran continuously, causing Gavin's tiny, one-pound frame to continually shake. Seeing a one-pound baby shaking from such a high rate of supported respirations was shocking, but his nurse assured me he was more stable now and moving to this particular machine was one of several things that had likely saved his life.

I clung to hope. There was no choice, but to just believe this could be done.

I stayed in the NICU a while, but when I could see all was as stable as it could be, I had them call my nurse to bring me back downstairs. We had a long journey ahead, and it was time to gather some strength.

Chapter 7

DESPITE HAVING JUST HAD A C-SECTION, there was no time to rest. The next day, it was time to focus and get to work on this NICU journey. I was allowed to shower, dressed in some of Brian's extra clothes, and after a couple more barefoot trips up and down to the NICU, I began to cringe thinking about what was under my feet so I had my nurse track down some gripped socks from another unit. My parents arrived back from Texas (where they had just returned home) and as I had expected, my mom had already constructed beautiful, hand-made banners with each child's name for their bulletin boards.

Although I kept trying to pump, no milk came. The day after the delivery, a gruff lactation consultant burst in, asked a quick permission, and gave me such a hard squeeze, I yelped in pain. I looked over at Brian who for once was speechless. I was about to stop her, declining any further help, when there it was – a tiny bead of milk trickled out. She grabbed a vial and bottled it, squeezing again. It was almost barbaric, but it worked. Soon I had learned the technique myself and was delivering a toothpick-sized vial of milk upstairs every three hours. The nurses on the mother/baby unit would always offer to take it for me, but it gave me a chance to check on the twins since I was still technically supposed to be spending my time downstairs recovering from surgery. I never did see this lactation consultant again. The other consultant I would work with over the next few months was soft-spoken and kind, but perhaps what I had needed to get the whole process started was a bit of tough love. The discomfort I had felt was nothing compared to what my son and daughter were experiencing upstairs. I ditched the wheelchair and began to walk to the elevator to build my stamina back. Brian came with me and also went up even more on his own between my trips. My doctor agreed to manage my post-op surgical pain with a non-narcotic medication so I could drive sooner and get myself to and from the NICU without restriction. Brian left and returned with a hospital-grade breast pump he had rented by the month since I would be exclusively pumping, as opposed to being able to nurse, for several months to come.

We were already deeply in love with our babies. I have heard stories of people who were afraid to allow themselves to unrestrictedly love micropreemies in the beginning because of the high risk of loss and I can understand this, but from the moment they were born, Brian and I were both all in. I was also quickly falling in love with our NICU and all of the staff. One of the neonatologists had been kind enough to give Brian a tour the day of the delivery so he could show me around now. I began to learn the routine of entering the NICU which was much different than walking into any other unit on the hospital. On this unit, even more than on others, germs were the enemy and even a cold could lead to the most unthinkable tragedy. The doors were locked and visitors stopped at the front desk to speak with the secretary and fill out a form each day that asked if you had any cold symptoms or if you had traveled. ID's were checked, badges were provided, and germ-transporting jewelry such as rings and watches were removed before the door would be unlocked. Before stepping further into the unit, there was a large washing station where you scrubbed for three minutes, up to your elbows as if you were preparing to go into surgery. Having had the twins so prematurely, fear of germs now consumed me, and I would scrub until my arms were pink.

It is almost impossible to describe a one-pound baby with only words. They were *so* small, unfathomably small. They could wrap all of their fingers around one of ours, and their hands wouldn't cover more than one of our fingernails. Their diapers were smaller than a box of cards. Their blood pressure cuffs were the size of a small Band-Aid and even then, it had to be wrapped multiple times – around their *legs*. As expected, their eyes remained fused and there was little movement other than what was provided by the ventilators. The small movements that did come from their arms and legs were quick and jerky as if their brains hadn't quite learned how to coordinate motion yet. Their nipples were so faint, they seemed to not exist. We were seeing babies that should have been tucked safely inside a womb for another *four months*, seeing development and changes occur before our eyes that most people could only read about in books. At even one pound, each baby had unique facial features. They had tiny eyelashes and miniature fingernails. Their beauty, their fragility, and the overwhelming love I had for these tiny beings made it hard to breathe. Their skin was paper thin with a purplish red tint. Gavin remained on the oscillator, sporting his yellow earmuff while his body trembled from the high rate of respirations. Both babies dozed under purple bilirubin lights wearing black blindfolds to protect their eyes. Some newborn photographs feature a wedding ring dangling from a plump baby toe; for our twins, a wedding band slipped over the entire foot. Their arms and legs were as thin as pinky fingers and there were small wrinkles in their skin, not because of the typical newborn baby fat but instead because there was just so little muscle and bone beneath it.

The pregnancy app I kept forgetting to delete informed me my newborns should resemble an ear of corn.

The rooms were kept dark and the whole row was kept quiet. Babies this premature were easily overstimulated, and this could lead to a drop in their oxygen levels or bradycardia, a sudden drop in heart rate. Blankets were draped over the top of each isolette to block out any remaining stimulation and to make the environment as womb-like as possible amidst millions of dollars of medical equipment.

The day after they were born, we were allowed to touch our babies for the first time. Our nurses taught us the process we would come to know by heart. We were told never to rub their skin, even gently, because it was so thin that it could tear. We learned to spray additional sanitizer on our hands, press a button on the isolette to prevent humidity from escaping, and then open a porthole. While the nurses used gloves, the parents did not so the babies could feel gentle touch which was vital because at this point, much of the touch they had felt involved pain. They had endured IV placements, intubation, and heel sticks to draw blood. At first, it was terrifying to touch them. I was so afraid we would overstimulate them or hurt them in some way. Soon, though, we began to realize our touch did not cause harm at all, and we slowly gained confidence. First, we nervously felt a tiny foot or hand and then, ever so gently, the top of a head. We learned which tubes and wires were not too concerning if jarred (pulse oximeter wire, temperature probe, blood pressure) and which ones to stay far away from (most importantly, the ventilator tubing coming out of the mouth).

Each baby was given a soft blanket loosely shaped into a head and body. These were provided by the hospital for the parents to sleep with and then return so they could be placed next to the baby, and the baby could smell the parents' scents. Brian brought them down from the NICU the day the twins were born and we each tucked one next to us that night. The next night, we traded and then we took them back up to the NICU. We watched as the nurses lovingly tucked them next to our son and daughter, usually close to their tiny heads so they could feel the softness and smell the scents of their parents. It was easy to let your mind wander into dangerous territory. What were the twins thinking, all alone enclosed in glass? Did they think their mother abandoned them? Did they miss their sibling? How much pain were they enduring from the barrage of tests and needle sticks required to keep them alive?

On the third day, the nurse stunned us. We were standing in room 3, peering down at Hannah when the nurse asked,

"Would you like to hold her?"

I couldn't believe it was possible. I had only touched her hands and feet and even that still made me nervous. Could she possibly be safe outside the protection of her isolette? What about germs? What about all of her wires and tubes? I didn't want to be selfish and have anything happen to her although, of course, I did desperately want to hold my baby.

"Is that okay? Only if it won't hurt her. I don't want to hurt her."

"It would be good for her."

The nurse explained that recent research had found that extremely premature infants actually have physical improvements, such as better oxygen saturation levels and fewer bradycardias, when they are experiencing what is referred to as kangaroo care, or skin-to-skin contact. Because of this, at our hospital, even the tiniest of micropreemies can begin kangaroo care as soon as possible. Being on a ventilator is not a restriction however being on an oscillator is so Gavin would have to graduate to the regular vent before his turn.

A team was assembled. Yes, a *team* is needed to simply hold a baby this premature. Most mothers are able to immediately take their newborns into their arms minutes after delivery; our plan required three medical professionals and military-like precision. My team, however, seemed thrilled to be doing so much work, and I realized how rewarding it must be to help a mother hold her baby, especially a sick baby, for the very first time. They pulled the curtain, blocking me off from the hallway, and had me take off my shirt so I was wearing only a bra. Babies this premature were not dressed in clothes, only a diaper, so Hannah was already prepared for her skin-to-skin touch. They directed me to the recliner where they pulled the lever and had the chair lay back with the footrest up. Hannah would need to be very still. There would be no rocking these babies for months.

There were two nurses and a respiratory therapist. One nurse held Hannah, whose head was now covered with the most beautiful ocean-colored turquoise and pink hat knitted for her by a volunteer.

Another nurse held an entire armful of wires and tubes while the respiratory therapist handled the ventilator and its critical tube into her lungs. They counted to three and moved with a surprising fluidity. Within seconds, I felt a tiny, diapered bottom resting in my hand, and Hannah's chest was on mine. She was facing the vent to my left, and the therapist began to tape down the vent tubing with medical tape. The nurses finished adjusting the wires and then covered us with multiple blankets so Hannah could maintain her body temperature outside the isolette. One of the nurses offered to snap a photo with Brian, Hannah, and I and then she handed me a large, handheld mirror. When I held it up, I could see Hannah's tiny face.

Just as quickly as they assembled, the team left. Brian and I were alone as I held our baby girl with our baby boy visible next door in his isolette. Hannah made tiny sucking sounds on her vent tubing and in the perfection of the moment, the hissing of the vent faded into the background. I was simply holding my baby. She could feel my skin for the first time and hear my heartbeat, the one she had heard from the inside for only six short months. I could finally show her Mommy was still here, that I hadn't abandoned her after all.

The research was right. I held Hannah for over thirty minutes the first day, and her oxygen levels and bradycardia episodes were better than when she was alone in her isolette.

The next day, since Hannah had tolerated the hold so well, we had the opportunity to hold her again. This time, it was Brian's turn. The team arrived and the same graceful transfer was completed. They set her bottom in Brian's palm, and she snuggled right in against his bare chest.

They were blanketed and taped. Then, like the previous day, the team left to give us privacy as a family. I alternated between watching Brian snuggle Hannah and watching Gavin in his isolette. At one point, I looked down at Hannah and did a double take.

"Brian, look! Look at her hand!"

He grabbed the mirror, concerned, and looked back at me for an explanation.

"She's making the sign language 'I love you!' "

Our tiny girl, barely over a pound with her eyes still fused, had raised her hand, the size of a thumbtack, up onto her daddy's chest and formed the sign where her third and fourth fingers were down and all others were up. "I love you" in American Sign Language.

Things were going to be okay. They had to be.

Chapter 8

2010

WE HAD BEEN TRYING TO BECOME PREGNANT for well over a year. One by one, our friends had all begun announcing pregnancies and even logging on to the computer had become depressing because every day, someone was thrilled to report their family was growing. I had undergone two surgeries, one by Dr. Barrett and another by a reproductive endocrinologist, removing multiple cysts, my right ovary, a fallopian tube, and adhesions. We did our first round of IVF and two embryos were implanted, but the pregnancy blood test was negative. The day I got the call, I came home, threw on my running shoes, and tore out of the house. I hadn't run in a very long time, trying to make my body as prepared as possible to accept what had appeared to be two perfect embryos. There was no longer any reason to rest and by the time I got home, drenched in sweat with my face streaming with tears, Brian had returned from work. He tried to find something to say, but he was just as devastated. We heard stories of unwanted pregnancies and of child abuse and neglect, and the unfairness of it all swept through me like a wave. In the end, it was the same drive that had now pushed me through three long-distance triathlons that would not allow us to quit. We chose to complete a second round of IVF.

Our countertops were littered with sharps containers, and our refrigerator had a shelf dedicated to vials of medication the size of your thumb that cost over a thousand dollars each. Every morning, we prepped my abdomen and Brian gave me shot after shot with as much gentleness as he could. I was exhausted, fighting the migraine headaches the medication caused, and unfocused. More than once, Brian raised an eyebrow as I handed him the prepped needle, nodding toward its flawed tip I hadn't even noticed that would have torn my skin and added to the pain. My stomach became an ugly collage of yellow, brown, and purple bruises, but we held on to hope that this was going to be *the* cycle. Every needle stick would be worth it to have a baby. At night, we did more injections, intramuscular ones with thick needles the length of a finger. Brian would inject these into the back of my hips, alternating sides each night, as I squeezed my eyes closed against the pain. I had knots beneath the muscles from so many injections. I went to the doctor every few days to have blood drawn and tested. My veins became difficult from so many draws in such a short period. I had to hope it would all be worth it in the end.

I was sedated for my second egg retrieval and once again, only around ten eggs were retrieved. They were sent to the lab, matched with sperm, and five embryos formed. Each day, the embryologist would call to provide an update on how many embryos we still had as it was a normal part of the process that not all the embryos would continue to progress. I took the final call while at work between patients.

"I'm so sorry to tell you this. There are no longer any viable embryos."

Chapter 9

WE KNEW THE TWINS WOULD likely be in the hospital until close to their due date four months away, but after three days, I was released to go home. The nurses offered a wheelchair, as that was the standard protocol for transporting post-partum mothers, but I had been walking to and from the NICU for two days so they allowed me to decline. Brian loaded a wheeled cart with all of the flowers and belongings I had accumulated in my days at the hospital, and we walked to the car he had pulled up to the door. It was a lonely feeling, going home after giving birth with no baby in a carseat, but not one to dwell on considering how much hope we had for our babies. In just the couple weeks I had been in the hospital, the weather had changed from warm spring to sweltering hot. The world had changed so monumentally in such a short period of time. The NICU nurses told me to call any time to check on the twins, even when I was up pumping in the middle of the night. We lived forty-five minutes from the hospital, and the staff made sure to tell us we were welcome to visit any time, day or night.

Since I came home on a Thursday, Brian and I were able to go to the NICU together for the next few days before he had to return to work. We were very hopeful everything would work out, and we wanted to save as much of his vacation time as we could for when the twins got to come home. We set up a breast pump station in our spare room where I pumped every three hours, day or night. We bought a deep freeze to store breast milk. I began poring through a book the size of an encyclopedia on loan from one of the social workers that detailed everything involved in the health and complications of being a micropreemie. It would be easy to become swept up in reading about all of the terrible things that could go wrong so I made a deal with myself to only read the sections with straight-forward, general micropreemie information. I decided to skip any sections on potential complications such as brain bleeds, intestinal tissue death, blindness, deafness, mental retardation, and long term ventilator support with the promise that I would only return to these sections if and when we actually met with that fate. I read and reread the list of successful former preemies: Picasso, Franklin Roosevelt, Mark Twain, Winston Churchill, Voltaire, Rousseau, Einstein. Actor Colin Farrell was born at 1 pound, 6 ounces. This was not impossible; we could do this.

When we visited the NICU, we discovered Dr. Barrett had returned and had been checking in on the twins. He had written encouraging notes on his script pad, leaving them in the room for us. Volunteers had stepped up to the call, and tiny crocheted hats began to appear in rooms 3 and 4, waiting to keep a one-pound miracle baby warm. The twins' beds were changed frequently, and it was so comforting and *normal* that beneath the unbelievably small babies and all of the tubing and wires, there were handmade felt blankets covered in pink cats and blue trains made by volunteers.

We began to adapt to the foreign language spoken in neonatal intensive care. We watched as doctors and nurses pored over the smallest details because at this stage, even the slightest infection was a mine field. Every diaper was weighed, vitals were checked, and lungs were evaluated by multiple chest x-rays each day. Our babies would have more diagnostic imaging in the first few weeks of life than most children would have in eighteen years. There were so many details to observe, so many calculations to be made, but really it all came down to one thing.

They had to breathe.

Their lungs were so premature and so underdeveloped that simply breathing, with the ventilator providing full support, was enough accomplishment each day. The doctors displayed the cloudy chest x-rays and we listened as the ventilators hissed and pulsed, praying for the twins to just hang on so their lungs could grow bigger and stronger. They were given caffeine to stimulate breathing. I joked that if I had drunk coffee while I was pregnant, maybe their lungs would be stronger. The nurse offered a sad smile and answered that she was glad I didn't because they could have been born even smaller.

Each baby had a complex monitoring system in the room. Oxygen level and heart rate were continually evaluated and a slow, warning alarm would sound if the oxygen level dipped below 85% or above 94%. Oxygen saturation in a micropreemie was a delicate balancing act. Too low and the baby was struggling to breathe and organs were not getting the oxygen they needed, but too high and there could be tissue damage as well. Retina damage. Blindness. Another frantic, high-pitched alert would ring out if oxygen dropped below 80%, if the baby's heart rate dropped, or if the baby had an episode of apnea when breathing temporarily stopped. If a baby hit the second, high-pitched alarm, a warning would show up on the monitors of all the babies in the area to alert the nurses in case the baby in distress did not have someone in the room to help. Our babies, as sweet as they were, monopolized the monitors. The alarms in rooms 3 and 4 did not stop. *Ever.* At the very least, both twins had a near constant warning alarm of 85% and then the high-pitched one would kick in for one of them every minute or so. When we were with one twin and an alert came up on the monitor, it quickly became habit to look up at the screen to check and almost without fail, it was our other twin with a desat or brady. They each had one-on-one nursing care, and the nurses were constantly bumping up the support on the ventilators when oxygen levels plummeted and adjusting the settings once again when they stabilized. Then the alarms would start up again. When we would go home after several hours, I would realize I'd been holding my breath the entire visit. None of us could rest or breathe peacefully.

Often when the alarms began to escalate, the nurses would reach into a porthole and firmly rub the baby on the back or side. They explained this was stimulation to alert the baby. The area of the brain that controls breathing is so underdeveloped in micropreemies, they often simply *forget* to breathe.

We were warned by everyone that the NICU journey for a micropreemie would be "a roller coaster." In even the first few days, this became obvious. The highs, such as touching a tiny foot or caressing a head that was still soft despite its miniature size, caused more joy than I ever could have imagined, making me ache with happiness. The lows, though, came hard and fast, leaving you grasping wildly for the lap bar to save you.

Gavin had made big strides. After several days on the oscillator, he was able to return to a regular ventilator. Despite the continual alerts from the monitors, his room seemed oddly quiet and empty without the bulky machine. His yellow earmuff was gone, and I noticed for the first time he was covered in lanugo, a very fine blonde hair over his entire body. The nurses called him their "California beach baby" as his hair appeared to be more strawberry blonde by the day. While his sister was having difficulty having her first poop, Gavin had skillfully learned to shoot poop all the way to the end of the isolette if an unsuspecting nurse was not quick enough on the diaper draw.

One day when we arrived in Gavin's room, we were greeted by a smiling blonde nurse named Allie. I had barely placed all of my pumping equipment in the chair when she asked if I would like to hold him. I started at her.

"Really?"

We had been restricted from holding him before by the oscillator, but even now, I hadn't figured he was stable enough, as he continued to desat often down into the 50% range. She assured us that it would be good for him and within minutes, I was settled into the chair, shirt off and fully reclined. A few minutes later, the tiniest, most perfect boy I could imagine snuggled onto my chest. The little boy who required chest compressions at birth to encourage his tiny heart to beat, the one who had battled courageously through that first night to fight for his life, was now resting skin-to-skin with his mother, snuggled under blankets, and satting reasonably well. Allie would tell me the next day how she had dinner with her fiancé's parents later that night and they had asked her about her job.

"I got to tell them I helped a mom hold her baby for the first time." She was *beaming* across the room as she said it, so obviously in love with her job and her tiny charges.

Even at night, we were kept informed. Sometimes it was more serious, such as news that one of the babies required yet another blood transfusion, but sometimes it was more playful such as, "You'll never believe it! Mr. Gavin has decided to open an eye!"

The blood transfusions became something of an odd phenomenon. Prior to the NICU, a blood transfusion would have been a really big deal to me. And in my newborn baby? Huge. In the scheme of things in the NICU, a blood transfusion is not the worst of things. When one of the twins would become anemic, they would become more lethargic and the numbers on the monitors would drop even lower. The doctors explained the rigid screening process for blood transfusions in general and then we were told how in the NICU, only blood from a very small percentage of donors who were approved for adults would be approved for these babies. It was the best of the best, and they used blood from the same donation as long as they could for each baby to minimize exposure. We were not allowed to donate our own blood, despite having family members volunteer, as our babies needed the blood now and the process to screen our blood would take too long.

After a transfusion, numbers went up and color returned so instead of being petrifying, a blood transfusion actually became a positive thing.

The twins' eyes began to open. The nurses got the privilege to see the first tiny squints on both kids. It was usually one eye at a time and it was like spotting a wild dolphin in the ocean; you had to be looking at the right place at the right time. Brian and I would watch intently and wait, knowing the nurse had gotten a good look just that morning. Over a couple days, the tiny peeks became a little more frequent until finally, both twins could look up at us with two squinted eyes and wrinkled foreheads as if they had been peacefully sleeping in the dark and someone had turned on all the lights. It was fascinating to watch them work to achieve each and every thing that comes so easily to a healthy newborn, something as simple as opening both eyes. They were beginning to take part in a world they should have only been hearing for another four months. Yes, machines were breathing for them, but despite being born so very early, their tiny bodies were trying to adapt. The level of fight in these preemies was astounding.

Brian and I began to learn how to help with the cares that were performed every three hours. We would reach through the portholes and take a temperature by placing the probe under an armpit, gently holding down the baby's arm. Their arms were no bigger than my small pinky finger, but if you want to see a demonstration of how hard a one-pound baby can fight, try to hold that tiny arm down for the minute or so it takes to get a temperature reading. Next was the diaper change. I had very limited experience in changing diapers on any baby and Brian was the same. Learning to change a baby at elbow height, from the side, around wires and tubes while reaching through two portholes was a big challenge at first. You couldn't be too slow about it or the baby's oxygen level and heart rate would begin to drop leading to a symphony of alarms. As with any new parent, though, we started to learn and soon, I knew which side of the isolette to move to because if it was tough right-handed, it was nearly impossible with the left. I learned to be more and more confident with touching the twins and less afraid they would shatter the instant I lifted their tiny bottoms to place a new diaper underneath. The nurses were never far away, but as we improved, they did not need to have their hands in the portholes on the other side to assist.

Hannah had a terrible time getting her first poop, another issue micropreemies can battle that a full-term baby never thinks twice about, and the doctors were getting concerned. We couldn't start putting any breast milk into her feeding tube until she pooped and while breast milk can be very beneficial to all babies, it is absolutely vital to micropreemies. They began giving her glycerin suppositories, but there were no changes. I happened to be standing with my hands inside the portholes changing her diaper one day when one of the doctors came by to check.

"Let's go ahead and order more glycerin."

"Wait! Taylor!" I called to Hannah's nurse for backup. Apparently, Hannah felt she'd have enough glycerin and all was working - and working- just fine now. Taylor grabbed gloves and was soon inside the opposite portholes as we went through diaper after diaper before the excitement stopped. Yet another silver lining of having a micropreemie; first baby blow-out and I had a nurse to help and a room full of people cheering.

Now that both babies had their GI systems working, they were allowed to try some breast milk. We were months from breast or bottle. Trying breast milk at this point involved placing about 1 milliliter of breast milk in a syringe taped to the top of the isolette and letting it slowly drain into each baby's feeding tube. To put it into perspective, this was one fifth of a teaspoon of milk to start, every three hours, so their main source of nutrition continued to be the TPN, nutrients fed intravenously. Before each feeding, the nurse would attach a syringe to the feeding tube and pull the syringe back, checking for any undigested milk or concerning colors. One of the biggest fears with micropreemies is necrotizing enterocolitis (NEC) which involves death of the intestines. It can easily be fatal and we would not be safe from this for months to come. Our twins showed no signs, thankfully, and feeds slowly began to increase to 2-3 milliliters while I continued to pump and stock our freezer.

Normally, when you go home with a newborn, your biggest fear is SIDS, and you do everything in your power to keep your baby on their back to sleep. Micropreemies are a different case. With regular ventilation guaranteed by the vent and constant monitoring, babies are often placed on their bellies. Many babies, ours included, love this and show better oxygen saturation in this position. We were constantly told to remember they should still be snuggled up inside me for another four months, and we had to simulate that in any way possible.

Brian and I were in the NICU one day and nothing seemed out of the ordinary, if you consider two one-pound babies on ventilators ordinary. We had helped with temperature checks and diaper changes, and Gavin's nurse turned him onto his belly. His warning alarm began as his oxygen dipped below 85% which was not that unusual. Then, the more urgent alarm rang out as he dipped below 80%. The nurse waited to see if he would bring himself back up and when he didn't, she adjusted some vent settings which usually led to stabilization within a few seconds.

He continued to drop.

And drop.

Unease shifted into terror. Until this point, all of our nurses had seemed calm in the face of crisis, but this nurse seemed frightened. She called out, panicked, for another nurse.

Gavin's oxygen dropped to 30%.

In my work as a physical therapist, I often help our pulmonary rehab therapist who works with adults who have diagnoses such as COPD and lung cancer. Many are on supplemental oxygen. We monitor their oxygen saturation levels with all activity, preferring them to be over 90%, watching them cautiously if they start to inch into the upper 80% region, and have them stop to rest and breathe if they fall into the lower 80% range. Gavin was 30%. He was about to code.

Suddenly, a wave of people descended upon room 4. Gavin's levels had sent out an alert to all the monitors in our section of the NICU and at 30%, anyone who possibly could was sprinting toward us. He couldn't get his oxygen level up, and it doesn't take long without oxygen to lead to brain damage and even worse.

We stood between Gavin and Hannah's rooms, moving aside for the doctors, respiratory therapists, nurse practitioners, nurses, and equipment. We could no longer see our little boy, but we could see on Hannah's monitor that his oxygen level was not improving. I was hysterical, frantically telling Brian, "it's still 30%, it's still 30%," unable to breathe myself; my baby boy was crashing and I could only stand by, completely helpless. Someone grabbed us and moved us out as they unhooked Gavin's breathing tube from the vent and hooked it to a bag they could manually inflate, forcing more air into his lungs during an emergency.

"Go to the parent room. We'll come get you."

They were not asking. They weren't going to allow us to watch him code. Somehow, Brian led me down the hallway, but I could barely see anything between my panic and the tears that blurred everything. He closed us in the parent room which is basically a lounge for parents to eat, watch TV, or just take a NICU breather. There was a father at the microwave who took one look at us and headed straight out the door.

Brian, ever the optimist, sat me down in a chair and repeatedly reassured me.

"He'll be okay. He'll be okay."

We waited, but no one came. Finally, Brian stood up and with a firm "don't go anywhere," he went to see what was happening. I sat alone in the parent room with my face buried in my hands, unable to think or move or even open my eyes.

When the door opened, it wasn't Brian. It was one of the nurse practitioners, and I felt everything collapse. It had to be bad if it was so serious Brian couldn't come back, if they were sending her in to tell me.

Her eyes opened wide and she rushed forward.

"No, no, no! He's okay! It's all right! He's okay now!"

It turned out, when he was turned onto his belly, the tube that connects to the vent dislodged in his airway and although the vent was running, he was not getting any oxygen support. Our newborn micropreemie basically had to try to breathe on his own, which was impossible. Once they checked the tube, it was obvious what had happened, they were able to reintubate him, and his numbers began to rise back up.

There had been a miscommunication and some nurses thought others were going to get us from the parent room and some who had run in to help didn't even know we were there in the first place. This particular nurse practitioner had been on her way out of the bathroom after the chaos subsided when Brian came running down the hall. She was so upset that we had been still waiting in the parent room that she ran down to get me herself.

When she told me he was okay, I completely fell apart as she sat patiently with her hand on my arm. Tears of relief, tears from the guilt I carried knowing my body was the reason the twins were suffering through all of this in the first place, tears of thankfulness for our little miracles, and tears for the fact that we were only several days in and we had months of these situations to go. I knew how important it was to be strong for our children. I knew it, and I was determined to do it. Sometimes, though, behind the closed door of the parent room, you break, if only for a minute.

Learning to Breathe

Chapter 10

2011

AFTER OUR SECOND FAILED IVF CYCLE, my doctor never bothered to call. Our credit cards had been charged, and apparently, they were just waiting to see if we would return to hand over another twelve thousand dollars for a third failure and further enjoyment of our doctor's atrocious bedside manner. Brian and I both realized it was time to take a break. We considered adoption, but at the time, approaching another unknown was too much for me. After years of trying and two failed IVF cycles, the idea of an adoption that could fall through at the last minute was not something I could even approach; I was not yet strong enough to handle that type of situation. Brian and I booked another trip to Mexico, our favorite place to get away, and decided that at least for now, we were happy just the two of us.

Then one day at work, I evaluated a new patient who had broken her ankle while she had been pregnant. With triplets. Having been through infertility and two rounds of IVF, when someone mentions multiples you can't help but wonder about their situation, always seeking out others who could understand the horror of the inability to become pregnant. We talked about her three babies and the situation with her ankle and as I prescribed her home exercise program, I never said a word about what I was really wondering. After seeing her for several weeks, she brought it up herself. She was single, in her thirties with no husband prospects as of yet, and she went across the state to a reproductive endocrinologist she had loved. After several more weeks, I told her enough of our story that she practically begged me to do a phone consultation with him. It would be free so nothing would be lost. My last physician charged over two hundred dollars for a consultation.

The doctor called me from his cell phone and we talked for nearly an hour. His attitude was that of "I like to pretend that with every patient, this is their one and only chance to do IVF so we have to do everything possible" which greatly differed from my last clinic which seemed to be "well, if this doesn't work, we'll try something different next time." Brian and I talked about it, waited a while, analyzed the financials, and eventually, we were on our way to St. Louis to coordinate our third round of IVF.

It was tricky going back and forth with four hours between our house and our new clinic, but Brian was allowed to do some of his work from our hotel and I traveled to as many of the checks as I could by myself. It often involved driving four hours, having a twenty minute appointment and one ultrasound, and then driving four hours back home but to us, it was worth it to be with a doctor we fully trusted.

His nurse, Sara, was training for her first marathon and we immediately became friends. We helped her with all of the advice on running we could manage and in return, she was practically always on-call for any questions or concerns that we had. Once again, we lined our countertops with individually packaged syringes, alcohol swabs, gauze, and sharps containers and moved the food in the refrigerator over once more to accommodate the tiny bottles of thousand dollar medication. The smell of antiseptic never seemed to truly leave my senses, and my abdomen once again became swollen and purplish black with bruising from the needle sticks.

I was so confident in this cycle and in this doctor that I was stunned at egg retrieval when there were only eight eggs retrieved. We drove home in near silence. We had to have faith. We had to hope there would be at least one good embryo and we would be going back to St. Louis in less than a week for a transfer.

About five days later at work, I got a call from Sara. I had learned from the last time and was now experienced enough in IVF failure to know to take the call in my car.

"I'm so sorry, Heather. There are no longer any viable embryos."

Chapter 11

THE NICU WILL LEAVE YOU in a constant state of emotional turmoil. It creates a phenomenon all its own, the ability to feel desperate terror and unspeakable joy at exactly the same moment. Every day, I closed my eyes and prayed, not just for the twins' health, but also that they would have no memory of this experience, of the needles, the heel sticks, the tubes down their throats, the pain. We continued to be allowed to hold both babies as long as they were not getting blood transfusions. Our family and friends enveloped us with support. There were prayer chains going throughout Missouri, Texas, and Utah. My parents visited frequently, bringing decorations and books, constantly trying to brighten the intensive care rooms of their tiny grandchildren. Friends brought food and cleaned our house. Two tiny crocheted hats arrived in the mail from one of my lifelong friends in Alabama. Food rolled in to stock our freezer; my aunt and uncle brought so much that they met us at the hospital and after they visited the twins, we went outside and they filled the entire cooler they had asked us to bring.

One of my childhood friends who lives overseas sent NICU care packages and each had a tiny blanket, a board book, a hat, and also parent survival supplies including hand sanitizer, gum, and snacks. Friends we know through Brian's work shared that their twelve-year-old had been born at 25 weeks, and they began walking us through every step of the way, telling us about their experiences, giving advice, and encouraging us that we could do this and so could the twins. They bought us a book about a duckling born much smaller than her brothers and sisters, but with time and patience, she, too, is able to spread her wings and fly.

We received stuffed animal music boxes from the parents of another childhood friend, a turtle and a lamb that played soft melodies with the twist of a key. When I opened them in my living room, the tears came again. They were touching, thoughtful gifts and I knew our children would love them, but they spoke to me so much because they were *baby gifts*. Yes, our kids were going to have huge medical needs and would have big fights to battle, but they also needed sweet, soft plush toys like any other baby. If you looked past all the medical equipment, wires, and tubes, they were still babies. To me, these music boxes showed faith that we would make it through this, and I could envision the twins snuggling them, not just at the hospital but also at home. My grandparents came to visit. My grandma had tears in her eyes as she peered inside the isolette, but there also may have been a trace of a smile. With the help of everyone around us, we were hanging on, taking one day at a time.

Then, suddenly, our NICU roller coaster plummeted.

We arrived at the NICU on one of the last mornings before Brian had to return to work. We knew they were doing another head ultrasound that day. These ultrasounds are done periodically on micropreemies in the early stages because they are at a high risk for what is called an intraventricular hemorrhage (IVH) which is bleeding in the brain due to the high pressures of oxygen required to keep them alive. Bleeding in the brain can lead to irreversible brain damage and profound disability. The twins' first head ultrasounds had been done the second day of life and were clear. One of our favorite nurses, Taylor, was working with Hannah when we arrived so I asked if they had completed the tests yet. Taylor, who was always open with us and one of the best at taking time to explain every detail to us about tests, procedures, wires, and numbers, only said,

"The doctor said she wants to talk with you this morning."

With just that sentence, I knew. Our roller coaster hadn't just dropped this time; it had veered off the track and erupted into flames. This was bad. This was very bad. As a physical therapist, I knew what could happen with bleeding in the brain, and I also knew that Taylor was not allowed to tell us anything, nor was it her responsibility to shoulder that burden even if it was allowed. But I also knew that if the tests had been clear, that was not the response I would have received.

When the doctor and nurse practitioner arrived, I was already in tears. They were compassionate and concerned, but also surprised.

"You're crying? Is everything okay?"

I managed to get out that I knew the need for her to talk to us was not good news. I knew the head ultrasounds were that morning. I knew what an IVH could mean. This was one of the times being in the healthcare field was a curse because a head ultrasound to me was not just another test. I had the knowledge and expertise to close my eyes and visualize how this could change the future for our children.

They pulled up chairs and encouraged us to sit down with them.

"As you know, the head ultrasounds were performed this morning. Let's start with Hannah."

"Intraventricular hemorrhages are rated grade one through four with four being the worst. Hannah has a grade two bleed on both sides of her brain which is considered somewhat mild. With a grade two, there is bleeding but not enough to move outside the ventricle, which is a cavity in the brain. We'll continue to repeat the ultrasounds to make sure the bleeding doesn't worsen, but if it stays at this level, we can't say for sure but hopefully, there may not be any long term damage. We've seen babies with grade two bleeds do very well."

"As you know, Gavin has always been the sicker baby."

I looked over at his isolette. He was resting, but occasionally, I'd see a tiny foot kick straight up into the air.

"Gavin also has a grade two bleed on his right side. But he has a grade four on his left."

Grade four. The most severe ranking of brain hemorrhage.

"Grade four means there is enough blood that it's pushing beyond the ventricle and is bleeding into the brain tissue itself."

Again, I looked at our tiny son resting beneath the protection of the glass, the image of pure innocence. He had no idea that at this very moment there was bleeding inside his skull, inside his brain, causing potential damage, and that possibly at this very second, it was robbing him of his ability to run or walk or talk or eat.

I felt myself fracture into a thousand pieces.

At this point, there was nothing the doctors could do except continual watching with more ultrasounds and placing a shunt in his brain to remove the fluid should it worsen and lead to hydrocephalus, an excessive build-up of fluid in his brain. Daily head circumference measurements were taken in micropreemies to watch for this swelling.

Once they knew we were able to handle the news, the doctor and nurse practitioner left to give us some privacy. A few minutes later, the NICU social worker assigned to us came in and sat down. We knew this diagnosis could mean anything from mild effects to very severe cerebral palsy. I would never allow a disability to lessen my love for my son and I was already vowing that he would have the best therapy I could find, but I was still devastated. I wanted both of my children to do anything they wanted, to be able to chase every dream, and there was absolutely nothing we could do to stop this grade four brain hemorrhage from potentially stealing these possibilities from Gavin.

Then the social worker looked me in the eyes.

"I've seen some kids grow up with a lot of problems and you don't really see much on paper. Then, I've seen some with medical histories like this and they are doing amazing. You can't just look at the history. You also have to take into account involved parents who are willing to do anything for their child."

That was it. There would be many more times in the future when I would shed tears over these bleeds, but no more paralysis from grief. If Hannah and Gavin could be strong and fight through all of this, then I could, too. It was time to extinguish the flaming roller coaster and climb back on board. I took out my preemie book and flipped back to the section on brain hemorrhage that I had skipped. I began to read.

Chapter 12

I TRIED TO MAINTAIN A POSITIVE attitude the best I could because it was the only way to make it through something so overwhelming, but as much as I tried to focus on the miracle it was that the twins were alive, there were moments that got dark. Very dark.

The news about the brain hemorrhages made me want to scream and throw the preemie book across the room. I became angry when I read books about other micropreemies and there would be sentences such as "but thank goodness, she didn't have a brain bleed." Round, glowing pregnant women, who used to make me uncontrollably jealous during our infertility journey, now made me feel hollow. Pregnant women who were doing things like running made me turn into a monster, angry at a world where women could run marathons and keep their babies inside and I simply walked around slowly and couldn't keep mine safe. Mainly, though, I felt rage and guilt at myself. Having a baby was central to being female and women had been doing this all throughout time in impoverished countries without medical care, yet my incompetent body not only couldn't become pregnant on its own, it then selfishly evicted two growing, perfect babies before they could even breathe. My mind reeled from all of the "if only" possibilities. If only we hadn't gone on that vacation when I was pregnant where I had done so much walking. If only I had eaten more so they had been even a little bit bigger. If only I hadn't run just a little bit when playing with a 5-year-old during her physical therapy. If only I hadn't taken that one shower the hospital had allowed me when I had sat in the shower seat for ten minutes the very day before the twins arrived. I knew they were meaningless, self-destructive thoughts, but there were times they couldn't be pushed away. Every day, though, I had to try. Thankfully, Brian remained optimistic whenever my emotions turned dark, and he could always make me smile, helping me to be once again ready to face the newest updates whether positive or bleak.

Brian had to go back to work and we began our new routine. I would get up, pump, get dressed, and do anything needed around the house and then head to the NICU. Brian would come to the hospital on his lunch break every day and kangaroo with whichever twin I was not holding, and we would alternate the next day. I began to feel more comfortable with the ICU rooms. I would now reach into the drawer beneath the isolette to get diapers or hats without first asking the nurse. I learned which hospital breast pumps were the good ones and which ones had wobbly wheels. My cousin's 3-year-old son colored pictures that I plastered on the twins' bulletin boards, further brightening their little rooms. I displayed books, stuffed animals, cards, anything positive I could. I finally deleted the pregnancy app on my phone that so kindly informed me that my now 25-week baby should resemble a rutabaga.

Our next hurdle was that both twins had a PDA, a patent ductus arteriosus. The ductus arteriosus is an artery that all babies have when developing in the womb that connects the aorta and the pulmonary artery. It is normal for this to be open in the womb because inside the mother, the lungs do not need blood. When a baby is born, this ductus closes within a few days, often with the first strong cries. In micropreemies, however, it is common that the ductus remains open ("patent") meaning extra blood from the aorta ends up in the pulmonary arteries putting pressure on immature lungs to work even harder. We knew immediately that both twins had a PDA as it can be heard through a stethoscope as a murmur. This was confirmed with echocardiograms completed right there in their isolettes. The plan was watchful waiting since some preemies are able to close the ductus on their own. There is a medication, indomethacin, which can be used to help close the PDA and after a couple weeks, it was decided Hannah would start the medication. Gavin, however, was not a candidate due to his grade four brain bleed since a potential side effect is increased bleeding.

While Hannah had her share of alarms, Gavin continued to have an even greater struggle. His white blood cell count went up and his oxygen levels fluctuated all over the place. He'd be at 90%, then steadily drop to 40-50%, then rise back up to 80% on his own. Blood gases were tested on both babies multiple times per day by sticking their heels with needles to draw out enough blood to measure the levels of oxygen and carbon dioxide, leaving them with patches of blood-spotted gauze nearly always stuck to their feet. Gavin's blood gases were worsening. His chest x-rays were cloudy. He was started on albuterol breathing treatments every six hours and the gases improved slightly, but not enough.

Even on the ventilator, he couldn't breathe. His oxygen regularly dropped to 40%. There was nothing we could do, but stand outside the glass and watch him struggle.

It wasn't long before a doctor came in to inform us of the team's decision. The PDA was beginning to cause serious problems with Gavin's lungs and it was time for surgery. Surprisingly, what I felt was instant relief which is not the emotion I would have expected to have upon hearing my one-pound baby needed heart surgery. He was suffering, though, and they had an answer and a plan that could fix it. The cardiac surgeon was contacted, and surgery was scheduled for a few days later. So far, the medication had not had any effect on Hannah's PDA so her surgery was set for a few days following Gavin's.

The day before the surgery, I sat in the recliner in Gavin's room as the team performed their graceful act of lifting our son with all of his lifelines and placing him on my chest so we could snuggle and talk. He had grown just enough that the endotracheal tube to his airway was now too small. The decision was to wait until he was under anesthesia to replace the tube so until then, the leak around the tube caused him to emit a small squeak with every breath. I told him to be brave and that the surgery would help him breathe so much better. I told him I wished I could have the surgery for him, but that he was in good hands and his mommy and daddy would be there waiting. Although micropreemies sleep most of the time, he was awake and alert for our talk, watching me with bright and innocent eyes, making the heart-wrenching squeak with every breath. Eventually, I knew he needed to rest so I stopped talking and simply held him until he slept.

The night before the surgery, a team wheeled Gavin's isolette down the hall and through a set of double doors to a different section of the NICU where there was a larger room used for surgery. The surgeon met with us to complete his pre-op exam on his tiny patient. He peered into the isolette and smiled as he made his notes.

"He's a cute little guy, isn't he?"

The day of the procedure, I was so thankful Gavin had Claire as his nurse; next to being an excellent nurse, she seemed to have a special place in her heart for Gavin. She had a young grandson also named Gavin who was only a little older than the twins and when we reached the operating room, she reached beneath her scrub top and showed me her necklace with her grandson's name engraved on it. She had chosen to wear it that day for our Gavin and his surgery.

Claire was busy preparing equipment, getting the forms we needed to sign, and making sure Gavin was relaxed and ready for surgery. Respiratory therapists were on hand, ready to oversee the ventilator. The doctor was running late from his previous surgery so while all the commotion continued around us, Brian and I had the chance to simply watch our son, who remained only a pound and a half, inside the isolette. There was morphine already dripping through his IV to keep the lights and commotion from startling him so he rested quietly without his typical jerky movements. He seemed at peace in his glass-enclosed isolation while everything moved so quickly around him. We heard murmurs that the surgeon was in house. Claire gently took my arm.

"We've got him. We'll take good care of him."

Brian took my hand as we walked out of the operating room, down the hallway, and through the double doors. I heard a click behind us and when I looked back, the double doors, which had been open every day during the three weeks we had been in the NICU, were closed.

Chapter 13

WE WAITED WITH HANNAH, who was sleeping quietly in her isolette. The curtain between the rooms was drawn so we did not have to stare at the emptiness of room 4, but it still looked hollow beneath the curtains with all of the equipment removed. The NICU seemed oddly quiet. We waited in near silence. Talk seemed almost offensive when a one-pound child was under anesthesia.

It had been under an hour when the doctor surprised us both and stepped into Hannah's room. The surgery was over more quickly than we had expected, and the big smile on his face told the story.

"He did great." He shook his head, smiling as if in disbelief. "He *really* needed that surgery. When we finish, we check the blood pressure to see if it has increased which shows if the surgery was successful. We hope for an increase of 4 mmHg. Gavin's increase was 26." He seemed blown away by this number.

I leapt out of the recliner, not knowing if I should shake his hand or pull him into a grateful hug so I went awkwardly somewhere in between, so thankful and relieved I could hardly speak.

We were allowed to see Gavin after some more time in recovery so we left a still sleeping Hannah, told her we would be right back after checking on her brother, and walked down the hall to the operating room.

Claire was busy, but she stopped to give us hugs when we arrived.

She raved about how well he did (which of course, she knew he would, being named Gavin and all), told us he was receiving morphine to control pain, and explained that he was puffy from the surgery which was expected. Her Gavin necklace caught the light as she moved around the room.

We peered in the isolette. His tiny back was covered in large bandages where the incision had been made. A chest tube wound its way out from beneath his incision. His entire body was indeed puffy, but only a little and beneath the swelling, there was our little boy and he was now resting, healing. Already his oxygen level had begun to improve. This had been the right call, and now our baby had one less obstacle in his path during his fight toward recovery.

They warned us he might get worse before he got better, but he never did. He steadily improved and after a few days of recovery in the surgical suite, they deemed him stable enough to be wheeled back down the hall into the room next to his sister, back to room 4.

"Oh, thank goodness," one of our regular housekeepers remarked when she saw he was back. "I was worried when his room was empty."

At first, I didn't understand. Then I realized what an abruptly vacated room often meant in the NICU, and I felt sick. I managed a weak smile.

"No, he just had surgery. He's okay."

We began preparing to repeat the entire process for Hannah's surgery. Although her alarms were not nearly as extreme as Gavin's, her oxygen desats were not improving and the medication had not affected the sound of her heart. It would be the same surgeon, the same routine, the same time spent down the hall in the operating room. Once again, I was talking to a baby the day before surgery, but this time, as I whispered to her, I could tell her how much it had helped her brother. I had seen the surgery succeed.

The night before her procedure, Brian and I were in the car and as he was pulling out of the driveway, my phone rang. NICU. It was one of the nurse practitioners.

"Are you sitting down?"

My heart dropped. At this stage in the NICU, there were too many possibilities to imagine, too many disasters we were trying to avert. I managed to get out a hesitant "yes." Brian glanced over with concern.

"Hannah's PDA is closed!"

"What?"

I couldn't seem to register what she said as she continued to speak. My mind reeled, trying to recover from the fear that she was about to tell me something horrible; it could hardly process that miraculously, our little girl's heart problem had abruptly resolved the night before her surgery. Yet, that was exactly what it had done.

"We did another echocardiogram tonight just to make sure and this time, it showed the PDA had closed. The medicine worked."

Add another miracle to our list. Another prayer answered.

"We canceled the surgery and told the surgeon she still has a murmur, which we'll watch, but it's not her PDA."

Now that we could all breathe, I told her how she terrified me by asking if I was sitting down and we were all able to laugh. She was just so shocked herself that it had happened. Our twins continued to amaze everyone, and you could almost imagine Hannah giving a little smile, knowing the impossible had been achieved once again.

Chapter 14

IT HAD BEEN THREE WEEKS. I wanted to be home with the twins for twelve full weeks when they came home from the hospital so I convinced my doctor to let me return to work for a few hours each morning. I had already informed my boss that my future plans had changed, and I would only be able to work eighteen hours a week instead of forty once the kids were home. I removed their names from day care wait lists and recruited my mom to watch them the two days I would work. They would not be able to withstand germs from other children in social settings like that for years.

My OB-GYN follow-up was with Dr. Barrett. We spent a few minutes on my exam and the rest of the time talking, with him apologizing for not being able to do my c-section and with me sharing photo after photo on my phone. He told me stories of micropreemies he had delivered who had beaten the odds. I told him about the brain bleeds and like the NICU doctors, he acknowledged the seriousness of the diagnosis but also told me to remember how resilient a baby's brain can be. He officially released me to drive which I had already been doing for three weeks.

Our new routine began. Brian and I both left for work early. I called the NICU on my way to work to find out which nurses the twins had that day, if there had been any changes overnight, and to check the twins' morning weights. I saw about four patients between 8:00 and noon, and then I hooked up my hands-free pumping bra and pumped while I typed patient notes in my treatment room. Then I would pack my milk into my cooler bag and head to the NICU where I would usually see Brian in passing as he continued to visit on his lunch breaks. Many days, I would arrive and find him still holding one of the twins in the recliner, sacrificing time to eat for an even longer hold. Every day, he held one twin at lunch and I held the other that afternoon and the next day, we would switch.

Being on the vents, holding time had to be coordinated with when the babies were fed, meaning when their special cocktail of breast milk plus high calorie formula was placed in a machine and run into the feeding tubes. The downside of this restriction was you had to coordinate when you could hold, but the huge upside, which far outweighed any negatives, was that once you were holding, you got to stay there for one to three hours. Despite the process it took to get the babies out of their isolettes, every single nurse seemed happy to do it. I'm sure their jobs are stressful and busy, but they never showed it to me. I learned that at many hospitals, babies on vents were not allowed to be held at all or only very rarely, and I felt blessed again to have been fortunate enough to be at this particular hospital. The NICU felt like home, and the doctors and nurses were starting to feel like friends.

I typed a letter that I passed out to each new patient at work explaining I had preemies in the hospital and asking them to please cancel their therapy sessions if they were ill. A cold in an adult could actually be the dreaded respiratory syncytial virus, or RSV, and if I passed this along, it would be very serious at the least and could be fatal at the worst. Thankfully, most patients' eyes widened when they heard how premature the twins were and none of them wanted to be the reason one got sick so they complied.

Our roller coaster chugged along. There was an incident when Gavin's oxygen levels crashed and the lowest I saw his oxygen saturation hit was 6% - practically none - but his nurse was calm and responded confidently, firmly calling another nurse to help without any panic, switching his endotracheal tube to the bag she could inflate to get oxygen in faster, and calmly calling the nurse practitioner to come, explaining "I'm bagging Mr. Evans." Nurse practitioners and doctors arrived and he stabilized; we never knew the reason for the episode other than "being a preemie." A few days later, they had to bag Hannah, but she, too, stabilized. I began to look at the NICU staff as angels and wondered what it must feel like to not just save a life every day, but sometimes every hour.

At one point, Brian was recording Gavin on his phone through the glass isolette. He was on his belly, wide awake, kicking his tiny legs. Suddenly, he raised his little bottom straight up in the air into a perfect downward dog position. Our tiny yoga master.

Although...not quite so tiny! The twins hit their two-pound goal right on schedule. An occupational therapist began coming to their rooms for stretching and positioning. Follow-up head ultrasounds revealed the brain bleeds were not worsening; the initial damage had been done, but if no further bleeding occurred and we could avoid hydrocephalus and shunt surgery, the damage would not worsen. At one month, the nurses used ink pads to stamp the twins' tiny footprints on decorative cards to hang on their bulletin boards. I brought them birthday cards changing "one year" to "one month." We were so completely in love with our babies and overwhelmingly proud of how hard they fought to live each day.

It had been about five weeks when I arrived at the NICU from work, toting my lunchbox full of breast milk, when I stopped in the hall, confused. There was a ventilator sitting there, draped in plastic, *outside* of Hannah's room.

I ran in to find the nurse practitioner waiting for me with a smile on her face, ready to see my reaction. I looked down at Hannah and sure enough, the tube down her throat was gone and in place, she had a CPAP mask over her face with large blue tubes running from it making her look like she was about to tackle a snorkeling expedition.

She was *off the vent.* Extubated.

The nurse practitioner cautioned me that this was just a trial. Her first setting on the new machine was called bipap which allowed some breaths to still be provided. Currently, it was set on ten breaths per minute which meant she was doing the other forty to fifty breaths on her own. The best part was now that the endotracheal tube was out, I could finally hear her voice. I had waited five weeks to hear my baby cry. On the vent, if the twins were upset, you could tell they were crying by watching their faces twist and contort, their mouths open, but there was no actual sound. Now, there was just the slightest, softest sound of a cry, almost like a squeak, and while you hate it that your child is crying, I couldn't help but love to hear what seemed to be world's smallest, but also most powerful, sound.

The next day, her blood gas reading was not that great. Her carbon dioxide level was up. The rate of respirations provided had been increased from ten to forty. Basically, she was maxing out the machine and was struggling even at that. The vent, which had never been moved from outside her room (now I understood why) was wheeled back in, and she was reintubated. We understood and were just thankful that she could rest now and did not have to battle so hard to breathe. No one was disappointed; it was a great try for a baby barely two pounds. Our neonatologist for the week felt she just needed to be bigger and the assignment for both twins for the upcoming week: "just grow."

We were back to slow and steady. At night, Brian and his dad took on remodeling our kitchen because he knew that would be out of the question once two infants were home. Occasionally, one of the twins would drop their hematocrit levels, which meant their red blood cells were low, and they would get yet another blood transfusion. Sometimes the IV's would be in their arms or legs, but often they were on their heads which was difficult to see as a parent. The nurses assured us this was actually an easy place for them to place the IV and it didn't cause them any additional pain, but it never stopped being a shock to see an IV piercing a baby's scalp. Every time, though, the twins would improve after the blood transfusion with better oxygen levels, pinker skin, and a more alert disposition so a scalp IV was a small price to pay.

Typically, night shift nurses gave the babies their baths, but when I asked if I could watch one night, our day nurse and her student volunteered to do one with me the next day. The main concern with bathing a micropreemie is efficiency. At times, even simple cares like a diaper change can cause a desat so a bath has to be well-prepared and fast. Our nurse gathered up the supplies beforehand – a stack of towels, new bed linens, a bucket of warm water, a small tube of soap, and some large cloth-like wipes. Being on the vent, there would be no submersion of a baby into a warm, sudsy tub. Instead, the isolette top was raised, the sides were dropped down and the babies were given baths right there in their beds.

Hannah went first. The levels of her vent were bumped up to give her higher oxygen support. The soft cloths were dipped in the warm, soapy water and she was gently cleaned head to toe around the essential tubes and lines that could not be removed. She was rinsed, and I held her up while the nurse swapped out the linens and then she was tucked back in. Hannah seemed to enjoy her bath. She watched us with alert eyes throughout the entire process and settled back in easily, wrapped in a blanket inside the warmth of her isolette.

Gavin was a different story. Typical little boy didn't want a bath. Unable to produce audible sound on the vent, he showed us his "crying face" the entire bath. It was more risky with him to remove the oximeter that monitored oxygen saturation. Despite the PDA surgery, he was still known to desat quickly and often, although this was much improved. Add to that his obvious agitation and a bath was a bit perilous. I stepped out of the way and the nurse and her student had him clean, dried, and warm within minutes and I was content to simply take photos. Sure enough, his pulse oximeter indicated a low oxygen level when it was placed back on his foot, but a quick bump up on the vent and a warm, cozy, closed isolette helped him to stabilize almost right away. A bath for a micropreemie, I realized, was almost a medical treatment with urgency and even risk, but there would be plenty of time for us to enjoy warm, soapy, leisurely soaks once the twins were healthier and at home.

Seven weeks into our stay, our friend Amy, who is a professional photographer, came for a session. When she found out I was pregnant, she had offered us a complimentary maternity shoot in order to build her portfolio. True to her word, she asked if I would still like the session despite the fact that my "baby bump" was instead two living, two-pound children on ventilators. I knew I wanted the session, and I tried to find the perfect time; too early and the twins were too fragile to risk something like a photo shoot but too late and I wouldn't capture this period. I definitely knew I wanted these first professional photographs to capture their incredibly small size, their fragility, the wires and electrodes, and the tubes and machines that helped them breathe because all of this was evidence of their miracle. This was their true story. I want them to be able to look at these moments and remember their strength and perseverance. Hopefully, they will see how beautiful life can be amidst fear of the unknown. These would be the images of two tiny beings who should not even be alive, and we wanted to celebrate our two-pound warriors.

For the session, I paired with Hannah and Brian paired with Gavin. Amy took shot after shot of us taking temperatures and changing diapers. She captured the angle through the isolette portholes and took close-ups of tiny feet draped in gauze. Her camera clicked as nurses raised the babies out of the isolettes with wires cascading down, she photographed as they were moved to our chests, and then she took endless photographs of us holding them, first alert and then asleep. She captured their tiny faces reflected in the hand mirror, she got the way Gavin's face was so small, a hospital-issued preemie size pacifier nearly covered him up to his eyes. She backed into the farthest corner of Gavin's room to take a shot of Brian holding Gavin in one recliner and me holding Hannah in the other, in two rooms partially separated by a glass door. With both twins attached to their ventilators, the recliners were probably twenty feet apart and yet this was our first full family photograph.

That evening, she sent me a message saying it was her favorite shoot of her career. While she had originally told me it would take several days for her to get the photos to me, she ended up sending an email late that evening. She had put other projects aside so she could edit and send the photos to me the same day, and she had even created a video montage. I cried through the video again and again. I brought it to the NICU. Nurses and social workers came in to watch, and many of them were brought to tears as well. Somehow, Amy had managed to weave the complexity of the equipment with the humanity of the fact that Hannah and Gavin were still, in fact, newborn babies. In some frames, the wires and monitors were harsh and highlighted while in others, they were faded to gray which directly mirrored how it felt to be in the NICU each day. Some days, it was hard to get past the numbers, the tubes, the fear, and the fact that each twin's entire existence depended on the competence of a ventilator. Yet on other days, things were more stable, they were just babies, and it was okay to plan for the future, okay to dream of nursery themes, and okay to think about the fact that one day they would come home.

Our family was with us for every step, every milestone. Since the twins had been born, my dad had secured a job an hour away and my parents were looking for a home halfway between his work and our house. They were wonderful grandparents already. My dad came armed with a camera and, always the scientist, asked the nurses questions and complimented them on their care. My mom decorated tiny teddy bears with the twins' names, kept the extended family informed, listened patiently to my daily updates, and started shopping for clothes and toys. It had been seven weeks and since no one except medical professionals and parents were allowed inside the portholes, they had not yet been able to touch their grandchildren.

Hannah and Gavin had reached the equivalent of 31 weeks gestation. After nearly two months in the hospital, they were still nine weeks premature.

Chapter 15

2012

I SAT ON OUR BED, staring at the wall in front of me, with my cell phone to my ear, listening to my doctor discuss our third IVF failure. We needed a break, mentally and financially, but I just needed to know what options, if any, remained. With each of my cycles, my one remaining ovary had produced only a small number of eggs. While that alone does not guarantee failure, in all of my cases it had not been enough to have success. He told me that if we planned to try one last time, our odds of pregnancy would be significantly increased by using an egg donor.

I hung up, and Brian and I took months to make our decision. I was worried how my child might react in the future when we shared about the egg donation however we also began to realize that without doing this, there would likely be no child to worry about at all. The donor would go through all of the hormone injections as well as the surgical egg retrieval so the cost was astronomical. This would only happen once so we had to pour all remaining hope into this one opportunity.

We chose an egg donor company and began carefully analyzing each donor. The first quality I knew I wanted was healthy, but we quickly realized donors were not accepted for the site if they had any health issues beyond eye glasses or seasonal allergies. I wanted someone who had previously donated with a good outcome. I needed someone who was open to meeting us in the future; even though the idea terrified me, I wanted it available if that was what my child chose when old enough to understand. From there, we chose our donor based on who we felt was the best fit for our family. The donor we selected seemed friendly in her answers, had a good relationship with her family, was dedicated to college, and had been active in a variety of activities. Many of her passions mirrored my own. I stared at her photographs, imagining the face of our future child. It felt as right as it could so we made the decision and before long, she began the injections.

Chapter 16

IT WAS TIME FOR BIPAP, round two. This time, Gavin would be along for the ride as well. Both twins now weighed in at a whopping three pounds which was much larger than Hannah's size at her first attempt off the vent, and the doctors felt we had a good chance this time. They also decided to use a round of steroids to help Gavin as he came off the vent. This was something we had been desperate to avoid as these particular steroids could affect his brain and possibly lead to developmental delays. Gavin already had his severe brain bleed and developmental issues are so commonly associated with a bleed of that level that the idea of adding increased risk and further damage to his brain was inconceivable to me. We drug our feet as long as we could, but then one of the doctors finally sat us down and explained that at this point, the risks of long term mechanical ventilation outweighed the risks of the steroid. The longer he was on the vent, the harder it would become for him to come off of it and being on the ventilator, while it was saving his life, could also be causing scarring in his lungs leading to lifelong dysfunction. The doctors had taken the decision very seriously. He told me they had discussed it at length in their meeting and it was a unanimous decision that this was the best choice. Despite their decision, we still had to give consent and as we signed the papers, I could only silently pray that we were doing the right thing for our son. I was already begging him to forgive me.

Hannah moved to bipap first, and it was obvious from the start that she was going to tolerate it much better this time. She had fewer desats, better blood gas readings, and required less work to be done by the machine since she was actively taking more breaths on her own. She was getting stronger and healthier every day and while we abstained from holds during this time to let her adjust and focus on her new increased work of breathing, we cheered her on through the glass of the isolette.

Gavin was next. He got his round of steroids and I tried not to think about it. I knew it was the right decision, but I still hated it. He was extubated and switched to bipap for the first time. Everyone held their breath...and he was fine. Maybe it was the steroids or maybe he was just ready, but the little boy who had been so sick and had required chest compressions at birth was now taking breaths on his own. If anything, his numbers actually improved off the vent, shocking us all.

Over the next few days, it became clear both twins had been ready to be off the vent. Their blood gases continued to be good and the alarm oscillations improved dramatically. On the same machine, the settings were changed to CPAP (pronounced SEE-pap). Now, no breaths would be given by the machine, requiring them to initiate each and every breath on their own. Again, we held our breath...and again, fine.

After a certain number of hours each day on CPAP, the nurses did what they called CPAP cares when the mask was removed and a bag was placed over the nose and mouth to ventilate. During this time, the nurses would massage the babies' heads where the masks had been. Being on CPAP caused them to have a puffy look and there would often be indentations on their heads and faces where the mask had been pressing, and the nurses would lovingly rub each mark. Most importantly for us, though, was that there would be a second or two when the nurses would pause after taking off the mask but before placing the bag so we could peer into our babies' faces unobstructed for just a split second. No tubes, no wires, just our son and daughter. And, once again, we were able to hear Hannah's tiny cries and for the first time, we were able to hear Gavin's small sounds as well. They were so delicate that when we would try to record them, they would not even be audible when played back.

One day, I was standing at the sink washing pumping equipment when one of the nurses asked me a question.

"Have they worn t-shirts yet?"

She might as well have asked me if they'd been to the moon, but knowing these kids, they'd try. Why on earth would my three-pound micropreemies have worn t-shirts? I must have been blankly staring at her because she turned to another nurse instead.

"Do you think they're ready?"

"Yeah, I don't see why not."

This is one of so many reasons why I love our nurses. While so many people in the world scrape by doing the bare minimum at their jobs, these nurses would take on extra work for themselves without question if it was good for the baby or the parents.

It turns out, a "t-shirt" in the NICU is a piece of light-weight, white cloth with arm holes. It is similar to a summer robe, and it is what is worn right before the transition to baby clothes. Medically, this is important because it is the first step toward moving toward an open "crib," the small glass bed used for full-term babies that is not covered on the top. To do this, the babies have to regulate their own body temperatures which is something micropreemies cannot initially do, thus leading to the temperature and humidity-controlled isolettes. While the twins' initial rainforest of humidity was now turned off, a warm temperature was still maintained in their isolettes and the kids were cozy in just their diapers. If they progressed to an open crib, they would need clothes to keep them warm, just like any other baby.

Non-medically, of course, it was also a good step because they both looked just completely adorable in their t-shirts.

Once in their t-shirts, the isolette temperature regulation was turned off and their body temperatures were checked more frequently. They maintained the appropriate numbers just fine so the nurse told me to go home and do laundry- I could bring in preemie clothes. I completed my assignment and the next day, we dressed the twins in their very first outfits, a turquoise onesie with a puppy for Hannah and a blue onesie with a monkey for Gavin. Tiny preemie onesies completely engulfed the twins, but the cuteness factor was almost too much to take. Past nurses came by to check them out in their new gear. A couple days later, Brian had the opportunity to dress one of the twins in a onesie during his lunch break due to a diaper incident. Let me just add here that dressing a preemie baby in a onesie through portholes with a CPAP mask on and various other tubes and wires exiting everywhere is *hard*. He was not as impressed with the onesie as I was.

"Why can't they just wear diapers again?"

Because the next day, I had a monkey sleeper ready for Hannah with a ruffle on the back and Gavin would be wearing sports with a football on the butt, and I couldn't *wait*. Oh, and that whole temperature regulation thing, too, I guess.

The preemie clothes were hard to top (for me, at least), but there was one other thing about the transition to CPAP that made it great. I was in Gavin's room, preparing for kangaroo care, when his nurse asked if I would like to hold him the other way. There had never been any other way. She didn't explain, but instead began to prepare. She took a blanket and swaddled Gavin into the shape of a small burrito with only his curious eyes and the CPAP mask peeking out. He looked around attentively, likely wondering what on earth was going on, having never been wrapped up in this way before. She then sat me in the chair, but when I reached back to recline, she stopped me for the first time ever. Instead, she placed a pillow under my elbow, adjusted the tubing, and placed my baby in my arms. I loved kangaroo care with the twins, but you had to use the mirror to catch a glimpse of their faces. Now, with Gavin as a small bundle in my arms, I could peer into his eyes and he could look right back, wide-eyed and curious.

"Hey, little buddy."

Most new mothers have the opportunity to cradle their babies this way and gaze at their tiny, perfect faces within seconds. I had waited nine weeks. There was no sadness or bitterness, though, only joy. We took nothing for granted. Every moment was a gift and while I still didn't understand why I had been blessed to be chosen to be the mother to these two miracles, I knew I would spend every day of the rest of my life trying to make myself worthy. Being in the NICU and in the micropreemie community, I had already heard so many heart-breaking stories of loss. You can never make sense of why one baby lives and another does not, but I knew that I would never take one single day, one minute, one second for granted again, and it would be impossible to ever see the world the way I had before. Our twins had been granted miracle after miracle, and I would be grateful for every smile, every hug, every step, and every milestone. I knew we still had a long journey ahead and the future remained very uncertain- we would not know the results of the brain bleeds and the steroids for years- but I could not have been any happier or more thankful. This was our family, our story, and it was amazing.

Chapter 17

2012- December

WHILE I HAD REGULARLY PRODUCED eight to ten eggs, our donor produced twenty. We never saw her, but we were at the clinic the same day she was and it was strange knowing she was in another room right down the hall. Several days later, instead of receiving yet another call that there were no longer any embryos, our doctor transferred the two best embryos into me and froze three others. The process took only a couple minutes. The doctor was smiling.

"You make my job easy."

I was wheeled out and laid flat on a stretcher so the embryos were not disturbed. Sara came in smiling, with two plates of homemade fudge and the first photo of the twins, a black and white picture of two circular embryos. I was advised to take it easy and we would know the result by a blood test in about a week.

As Brian drove us home, I laid my seat back as horizontal as I safely could. Over the next few days, I was allowed to gently move around but I downright refused other than to get up to go to the bathroom. The day before the blood test, there was a small bit of hope forming. Already, I felt just a slight bit off, just the tiniest bit nauseous, but I tried to tell myself it was just nerves. The day of the blood test, I was even more hopeful; I didn't feel bad, just not quite like myself. A few hours later, I got the email from Sara.

"Don't sign up for any triathlons or marathons this year-congratulations!"

Chapter 18

I WAS BACK TO THINKING about preemie clothes. I had to exchange some of the sleepers we had been given because they had zippers up the front. Zippers do not work for babies in the NICU as they do not leave room for wires and tubes to escape, something I never would have considered before embarking on this journey. The nurses warned us to be wary of buying zipped sleepers up to even 6-month-old clothes since the twins would likely leave the hospital on oxygen and apnea monitors. Special consideration had to be taken as we began to buy all the supplies we would need at home. When stroller shopping, we had to make sure the basket at the base would be large enough to hold two tanks of oxygen and two monitors. Carseats should be able to hold a four-pound baby. Bottles should be specific ones as there was a high likelihood the twins would have reflux. My cousin and I went to a massive children's consignment sale and I filled a trash bag full of what were (adorable) complete guesses. While I know many babies don't follow the designated categories of "newborn," "0-3 months," "3-6 months" and so forth, our kids would not even be close. I had no clue what to predict for, say, Christmas pajamas or what size they might need for spring and summer clothes, but that didn't stop me from attempting.

Several of our friends had said early on that they would like to host a baby shower for us whenever we felt we were ready. By August, once the twins were two months old, we felt we were comfortable with it so a date was set and I headed to the baby stores to complete the registries I had barely started before bedrest. It was almost funny to watch the poor cashiers retrieve the scanner for me when I told them it was for my shower, it was for twins and my due date was October 6th. Here it was, August, and I was supposedly 32 weeks pregnant with no sign of any kind of a baby bump. At one store, the girl was very friendly so I shared our story with her when I saw her obvious confusion. At another store, the employee was less than friendly so I just took my scanner and let her wonder. Maybe it crossed her mind that with such a lack of a bump, I was going to have very small babies. She had no idea.

Our friends hosted a stunning shower. It was a couple's shower so all of our friends were there to celebrate. A colorful cake with a caterpillar stretched along the countertop amidst rooms filled with food, fresh flowers, mountains of cards and gifts for the twins. Everyone asked for the most recent updates and praised the babies for how far they'd come. Our IVF nurse, Sara, and her husband drove in four hours, bringing additional treats she snuck into our car, taking time out of their lives to spend time with a group of people they had never met, to celebrate the twins. Though we kept in touch online, the last time I had actually seen her was on transfer day when she'd left me with the photo of our two embryos.

We left feeling completely loved by all of our friends. We basked in the warm glow; somehow, being around a group of such positive people and being so lifted up in support rejuvenated our faith that everything was going to be okay.

Our routine continued. One day, on my way from work to the hospital, I received a text from Brian. I checked it at the stoplight as I waited to turn into the hospital.

"Surprise!"

It was a photo of Hannah. *On nasal cannula.*

Her snorkel-like CPAP mask was gone and had been replaced with a singular tube running beneath her nose delivering a high-flow rate of oxygen. The doctors had felt she was ready to try intervals alternating between high-flow nasal cannula for six hours and CPAP for six hours. Moving to nasal cannula was yet another step down in the level of oxygen support, moving toward eventually needing none at all. They took a blood gas reading and it was stellar so they moved her to nine hours on the cannula and three hours on the CPAP. She continued to earn gold stars on her blood gases so they moved her to full-time high-flow nasal cannula, and she settled in just fine. It was remarkable to only have one tube beneath her nose even if the high-flow tube was larger than typical nasal cannula tubes. No more vent, no more CPAP mask obstructing her features. Within a few days, the puffiness in her face caused by the CPAP melted away. She was doing so well, they moved her to an open crib. Suddenly, there was she was for us, no longer separated by glass. We could hear her tiny baby sounds without pressing our ears to an open porthole. We could (douse with sanitizer and then) touch her without unlatching any doors. We could dress her and change her diapers with what seemed like unimaginable freedom. We could talk to her and read to her in bed without wondering if she could hear us.

Gavin began a rotation of six hours on high-flow nasal cannula and six hours on CPAP. The first night, he was completely spent and went back to CPAP full-time, but within a few days, he had gained strength and was on continuous high-flow nasal cannula, just like his sister. He, too, moved to an open crib. We had been in the NICU for ten weeks, and things were beginning to fall into place for the twins. Every day, we watched other babies and their families complete their NICU stays and go home. Although all of these babies arrived after us and left before, I never felt sad about it once. The NICU felt like home for now, and I was happy to stay as long as we needed to make sure the twins were as stable as possible before it was up to us on our own.

My mom finally got to hold one of her grandchildren for the first time. She was visiting with one of her friends when Gavin's nurse surprised us all and asked if she would like to hold him now that he was on nasal cannula. I'm fairly certain my mom was as terrified as she was excited, but his nurse was wonderful, assuring her he would be fine and telling her, "Remember, it's *my* job to take care of him and make sure he's okay. You just enjoy him." I was sitting across from her in Hannah's room with Hannah snuggled in my lap when the nurse placed Gavin in my mom's arms. Despite being a retired teacher who is a natural with children, it was obvious she was nervous and afraid to move while holding such a fragile baby. After a few minutes, though, she settled in and relaxed. Not many grandmas look at their grandchildren for ten weeks before holding them in their lap, but when Gavin was ready, she was there.

My grandparents came to visit again. The last time they visited, the twins only weighed a pound and were very sick. I remember how my grandma had tears in her eyes, although I feel they were at least partially happy ones, when she peered through the glass. Now, both kids were big four-pounders, in baby clothes and hats, in open cribs, and with only oxygen tubes beneath their noses for support. At this point, without question, her tears were ones of joy. They stood over each open crib, talking to the twins and pointing out what they had been unable to notice the first time, like Hannah's button nose and Gavin's silky blonde hair. They had been the first ones to start a prayer chain when I was on antepartum and they had kept these chains going strong, calling in for reinforcements when breathing was a struggle and before Gavin's surgery. Now, they could finally see what appeared to be the start of their answered prayers.

The NICU experience continued to bring about situations that should have, in theory, been completely unable to occur simultaneously. We had to let go of control and have blind faith in the doctors and nurses who cared for our babies while we were away. There was no choice but to believe in their abilities, their skills, their decisions, and their competency. Concurrently, we had to remain attentive and assertive, pushing aside any need to protect others' feelings when it came to what was best for our children. Sometimes a parent's intuition is even more valuable than all of the professional assessments. I went to one of the doctors when I disagreed with the way Hannah's foot was wrapped, leading it to be swollen, probably frustrating a nurse but as I had thought, the best care for our daughter involved rewrapping the foot with less tension. We felt one nurse was not a good match for our children, handling Gavin too roughly, and without any discussion, Brian pulled open the curtain, left the room and spoke to the charge nurse who reassigned her in the middle of a shift. We were respected and our opinions were valued. The doctors and nurses continually emphasized that despite the fact that the twins were hospitalized and under their care, Hannah and Gavin were still *our* babies and we had the right to be involved in every aspect of their treatment. They made it very clear from the start that we would be the ones who knew our babies best and that we should always feel comfortable letting the medical professionals know if we felt something wasn't quite right. While nurses and neonatologists changed shifts, we were there every single day. Several times, we noticed when something in one of the twins seemed off- eyes that looked too tired, skin that seemed pale, one of the babies was too lethargic, an increase in drops of oxygen saturation. The doctors never questioned us and they would order tests. On several occasions, the tests revealed infection or anemia, requiring antibiotics or a blood transfusion. We worked as a team. Supposedly, it takes a village to raise children. In our case, it was a village that saved ours.

Being in the NICU so long, I overhead hushed talk between social workers and other staff, discussing conversations with some NICU parents reminding them of the importance of spending time with their babies in the hospital. The idea of a baby alone in the NICU without parents doing their best to be there broke my heart. I spoke with some NICU parents whose homes were hours away. Some paid to lodge near the NICU, others traveled back and forth the best they could. Again, I felt blessed we were within forty-five minutes of the hospital and realized how much more difficult our situation could be. I met women who had c-sections in a hospital an hour away. Their babies had been whisked away to our hospital while the mothers could do nothing but remain in a different city while they recovered from surgery. I thought back to my barefoot treks upstairs in the middle of the night with one hand clutching a vial that contained a few precious cc's of breast milk and the other hand carrying my catheter bag and was thankful. No matter how traumatic our situation, it all could have been so much worse.

As the twins' oxygen support decreased, we began to see less of the respiratory therapists we had come to love. Being on the vent, we had gotten to know them well as one was always present to move us to and from kangaroo care plus they had to stop by at regular intervals to record vent settings. One therapist seemed to form a special bond with Gavin. He would talk to him while he was in the room, even when Gavin was enclosed in the full isolette. One time, I heard him say Mommy needed to bring in more books because they had already read all of the ones in the room. I'm fairly sure it's not in the job description of a respiratory therapist to read to a micropreemie, but that didn't stop it from happening. I was continually amazed at the size of these people's hearts.

The brain bleeds were stable. Monthly eye exams had been clear of retinopathy of prematurity, a very common eye condition in micropreemies. The PDA's were resolved although Hannah still had a slight heart murmur. We used to see the doctors early, first thing in the morning, and now they did not round on the twins until lunchtime. We learned this was because they always round on the sickest, most fragile babies first and the more stable babies later. We had been the first stop on rounds for a *long* time.

And then, one test came back a little strange. Hannah's direct bilirubin levels were high. Bilirubin is a product that is formed from the replacement of red blood cells, and elevation in even later term preemies is common. Both twins had elevated bilirubin immediately after birth and were placed under the bright purple "bili" lights to resolve it. This elevated bilirubin can be dangerous, leading to potential blindness, cerebral palsy, and brain damage, however it is easily treated in medically advanced countries with light therapy which eliminates any residual effects. This elevated level had been resolved for the twins months ago and in the list of concerning conditions they had, it was at the very bottom. Now, though, the elevation of Hannah's direct bilirubin was much more concerning. Direct bilirubin is made when sugars attach to bilirubin, and elevation does not typically occur even in preemies without another problem such as neonatal hepatitis. In fact, it was so odd that the first step was running the labs again as the doctors figured it must have been a lab error. It still came high. In fact, it came back higher. They drew a liver panel to check for the diseases CMV and hepatitis. They did ultrasounds of her liver and gall bladder. They tried to straight catheterize her to get a urine sample to test for a UTI, but they were still unsuccessful after three attempts. Two medicines, actigall and phenobarbital, were started to bring her levels down. They redrew blood after being on the meds, but the levels rose again. The worst part, other than that there was something wrong and our daughter was undergoing a battery of tests, was that many of these tests took a week or more to get back so we were left worrying about all of the possibilities with no answers coming any time soon.

Next came something called a HIDA (hepatobiliary) scan. A radioactive dye was injected, and they transported her in her bed downstairs to radiology and back up all day doing scans to see if her liver and gall bladder were secreting properly. All of the scans and movement completely wore her out. She slept through all of our visits. We couldn't hold her. They drew more blood to test for Down syndrome, alpha-1 anti-trypsin deficiency, and cystic fibrosis.

Then we waited. We waited for the local children's hospital to review the HIDA scan. We waited for the lab to grow more cells to get a conclusive result on Down syndrome. There was no section in the preemie book on elevated direct bilirubin.

Slowly, the results came ticking in. HIDA scan – normal. Down syndrome – normal. Alpha-1 anti-trypsin – normal. CF – normal. Our doctors began to think it was cholestatic jaundice which is basically just high direct bilirubin caused by being on TPN, the IV nutrient source, for so long. They redrew more blood and this time, after being on the medicine longer, her bilirubin level was finally starting to fall. We all breathed a collective sigh of relief. They weren't certain yet, but at least the number of tests (meaning the number of times our baby was pierced with needles to draw blood) was going down.

Amidst the bilirubin madness, the doctors decided the twins were ready to begin breast feeding. Their feeding tubes were moved from their mouths to their noses so they could latch better to breast and bottle. In the beginning, it is not expected that micropreemies will get a full meal with breast feeding alone. To start, a couple successful latches are a huge success. Both twins were able to latch three or four times on the first try before they settled in for their full meals provided in the feeding tubes. The nurses praised their efforts and both babies immediately passed out, exhausted from the effort of trying to latch, sleeping as breast milk and high calorie formula drained into their stomachs.

Our roller coaster twisted along its serpentine path. We went up: both twins moved to low-flow nasal cannula at ½ liter 100% oxygen which was the type of oxygen they would use at home. Then we tumbled back down: an echocardiogram showed the cause of Hannah's mysterious non-PDA-related murmur was in fact pulmonary valve stenosis, a heart condition in which one of her valves was narrowed. The children's hospital reviewed her results and determined no treatment was needed at this time however she would start her follow-ups with them beginning the first week of discharge from the NICU. The most absurd part was that it had nothing to do with being premature. This was a heart defect she would have been born with even if she had been full-term. It seemed brutally unfair that she would have this condition on top of all the micropreemie complications, but it was also ironic that the reason the heart condition had been detected so early was because she was so closely monitored due to her prematurity. There was nothing we could do except let them monitor her and trust their advice, continuing to take each day at a time, breathing in and breathing out.

Chapter 19

2013 – January

MY FIRST PREGNANCY OB-GYN appointment was with Dr. Barrett and he seemed as over the moon as we were. As standard procedure, I had a blood test to make sure everything was progressing as it should be, and he called me from his cell phone later that day.

"Well, you're definitely pregnant. Your HCG numbers are much higher than I expected."

"What does that mean? Is that good?"

"It means there's a high chance you could be having twins."

Chapter 20

THE TWINS WERE THREE MONTHS OLD and six pounds. *Six.* The size of a full-term newborn. They seemed massive; when your babies start out at one pound, your perspective is so skewed that six pounds seems like the size of a three-year-old. The social worker arrived one day and said she had something she needed to discuss. She talked about how well the twins were doing and said there were some mothers on antepartum that might be delivering very sick babies soon. The rooms we were in were typically used for the sickest babies, and they were wondering how we felt about moving rooms. We would have the same nurses and doctors, and they could put the twins in rooms across from each other. This was fine with us and when I told her that, she gave an audible sigh of relief which made me wonder if other families had not always been so agreeable. To us, it was just another step toward going home.

The next day, they excitedly informed us they would be able to move us to what they thought was the best room in the NICU. It was set up for twins so both babies could actually be in the same room which was even better than expected. I was prepared to help move all of the clothes, pictures, books, and stuffed animals we had accumulated, but when I arrived the next day, the twins had already been moved. I scrubbed in and headed to our new room. It was only about three rooms down from the surgical suite and I couldn't help but cautiously glance in that direction, but our time there already felt far in the past. I stepped into our new room. It was gigantic. Both babies were resting comfortably in their beds with two large recliners next to them. Off to the side, there was a couch with a curtain I could pull to have privacy while pumping. One of the nurses had arranged all of the pictures and toys, even tacking things up on the bulletin boards for us. I could sit in the chair in the middle of the room and look to the right to watch Gavin and to the left to watch Hannah. When the nurse tentatively asked what I thought, I almost hugged her. We would be happy here until we could go home.

It was time to get serious about this eating thing. Preemies have a much harder time coordinating "suck, swallow, breathe" than full-term babies. They were given their first bottles of breast milk and they did okay. To make it as easy for them as possible, they were bottle fed while lying on their sides. One day, Gavin managed to nurse for twenty-five minutes. They were still not consuming anywhere near the calories they needed in these ways so each time after bottle or breast feeding, they finished the remaining milk through the feeding tubes. Pacifiers were encouraged and even used by our speech therapist as a tool to promote a strong suck. The twins ate every three hours, thirty minutes apart, so this began our new routine. Brian would arrive at lunch and try to bottle feed one twin. Once eating stopped or the thirty minute limit was reached (after which point, more calories were burned than taken in), the tube feeding started and Brian would continue to hold until the feeding was complete and his lunch break was over. About that time, I would arrive from work and try to nurse the other twin followed by the same tube feeding/snuggle routine. I would stay and three hours later, I would nurse the opposite twin and bottle feed the one I nursed earlier since my milk supply was never high enough to feed both babies. The next day, Brian would arrive to bottle feed at lunch and our routine would begin again. We had the logistics down to a science, but the twins continued to struggle, especially with the bottles. Often, they would fall asleep and be too tired to eat. Sometimes, much of their meal spilled out the side of their cheek onto the pillowcase. They both had severe reflux and would often lose all the calories they had just managed to get down. The doctors reassured us this was what they expected for micropreemies and reminded us that they were not going hungry, thanks to the tube feedings. It would just take time, patience, and a lot of work.

In the meantime, we retired all of the preemie clothes and moved on to newborn. I packed up the preemie sleepers and onesies and placed them in a sealed container that I would not open again for a year because of the strong emotional pull it had. I put Gavin in the striped sleeper with tigers on the feet that I had used to announce my pregnancy to Brian. We hit the 100 day mark in the NICU. I ordered decals for the walls of our nursery at home, and Brian painted the room. There had been murmurs of discharge in a few weeks, but no solid predictions could be made until our feeding situation began to improve. Like many full-term babies, the twins lost some hair and more returned. In fact, being born so early, Gavin lost his hair twice going from blonde with a touch of red to brown and then to straight blonde.

I was blessed with another baby shower, this time for the women in my family. I walked in and was surprised to find the room filled not just with my own family but even with friends of my mom and grandmother. There were two diaper cakes, multiple banners and signs, baby outfits suspended from clotheslines, a cake decorated in both pink and blue, food, mountains of gifts, and so many people. In the center of the food table was a watermelon my uncle had carved into the shape of a baby carriage with two clementines decorated with eyes and pacifiers to represent the twins. He had carved wheels and surrounded the "babies" with an assortment of fresh fruit. The Hannah clementine even sported a pink bow. As I unwrapped blankets and books, while we pondered over the number of baby socks in a container, and as I watched my grandpa and dad arrive to help empty trash cans and wipe down tables, everything felt warm and safe. This family was our team. All of these people had kept faith from the beginning that the twins were going to live and be okay. As Hannah and Gavin lay sleeping in the NICU, I hoped they could feel it, the love of their family even from people who would likely not be able to meet them for close to a year due to the lockdown restrictions we already knew we would have.

Back in the NICU, the twins continued to work on eating. I loved our new room and having both twins right next to me in open cribs where I could really see and interact with them. If I arrived and one of the twins was fussing, I was now allowed to actually pick my baby up (carefully, as there were still oxygen tubes and wires tethering them to the wall) and move to a chair to gently rock. Holds were no longer restricted to feeding times alone since the babies were stable enough that getting in and out of bed was no longer overstimulating and exhausting for them. Often, the nurse assigned to the twins would also be assigned to another baby in the same hall. We had come a long way from one-on-one care with the nurse unable to leave the bedside. There were still alarms, but not often, and typically, it was just the first alert as opposed to the higher-pitched urgent alarm the twins used to favor.

One day, our nurse had our twins and another set of twins in the room next door who were healthy and about to go home. The mother in the other room was in the recliner with a chest full of babies, holding both twins at once. Our nurse came back into our room.

"You've done that, right?"

I hadn't figured it was possible with all of the tubes and wires we still had, but when I said I hadn't, she said she felt they were doing well enough to try.

I sat in the recliner between the two beds, and she placed one baby and then another on my chest with Gavin on my right and Hannah on my left, letting their wires trail off to both sides. After spending six months next to one another on the inside of my body and then three months abruptly stripped apart, the twins were finally back together where it all began- brother and sister together, listening to my heartbeat.

Our nurse took pictures for us as the twins gazed at each other with sleepy but curious eyes. I could feel their weight and warmth on my chest. I remembered when we first started kangaroo care holds, I could barely feel I was holding any weight at all, and now here they were, actually making my arms tired trying to support their weight. They drifted in and out of sleep, and we stayed this way for a while before the nurse came to help us back. Mothers of nearly full-term twins can hold both babies either instantly or after a quick NICU check. It had taken us over a hundred days and it would be another month before we could do it again, but at least for a few minutes, the twins had been reunited.

The end of September approached, and the generosity toward NICU babies continued. Blankets, pajamas, and pacifiers attached to stuffed animals appeared in the twins' room, gifts from previous NICU parents. One day, I arrived to find the twins in pastel bouncy seats that played quiet music. They had been donated to the NICU by twin boys doing their bar mitzvah service project. They had been in the NICU as babies and had raised a large sum of money to purchase an entire roomful of supplies for the unit. Hannah and Gavin loved the bouncers so much, we bought two for home. The love that surrounded the NICU was astonishing, and I looked forward to being a former NICU parent who could give back.

Hannah and Gavin began to take in more at their feedings, and there were more whispers about discharge. At night, Brian and I finished preparing the nursery. Brian built the cribs our parents had bought, hung mobiles and applied decals while I attached cherry blossoms to their wall and hung the framed canvases with their names, birthdays, and size. I wondered if it was the first time our artist had ever made a canvas with 1 pound, 9 ounces as the weight. Did she have to read my instructions twice to make sure she had read the weights correctly? Brian's father built a dresser with tiny animals for the handles, and I filled it with newborn clothes, blankets, socks, and hats. We bought a glider and borrowed a changing table. In our decorating, we made sure to figure in room for an oxygen concentrator.

Chapter 21

THE SEASONS BEGAN TO CHANGE. There was a new crispness in the air. I was now cuddling the twins in jeans and sweatshirts instead of shorts and tank tops. I had sprinted out to my car from the hospital in pouring rain as darkness arrived sooner each night. Autumn had arrived, and it was hard to believe we had been in the hospital since the very beginning of summer.

My mom brought us "preemie pumpkins." She had taken small pumpkins and drawn on eyes, decorating them with hats and pacifiers. I ordered two crocheted baby hats for Halloween – Little Red Riding Hood (complete with two long braids) and the wolf- not knowing whether the twins would wear them at home or in the hospital, but they needed costumes for their first Halloween either way.

We knew home was in the near future when the doctors decided it was time to get the twins into normal safe-sleeping positions. No more sleeping on their bellies, no more blankets in bed. I brought in their new sleep sacks, and we started securing them inside, on their backs, with nothing else in the crib except a pacifier, the oxygen tubing, and the remaining wires.

We felt like we were nearing the finish line when, in typical NICU fashion, everything changed and we came to a grinding halt. Gavin became congested and anemic, requiring yet another blood transfusion. The speech therapist fed Gavin a bottle and was concerned about him choking and letting milk run out the side of his mouth. She ordered a swallow study, a test where imaging is completed while he is drinking and, as she expected, the breast milk I had so painstakingly pumped was going down more quickly than he could coordinate a swallow. He was aspirating it into his lungs. The test continued, this time with straight formula which is slightly thicker than breast milk, but again, aspiration. Hannah was tested the next day with the same result. So after all of the diligent pumping with a focus on how breast milk is so vital to preemies, the twins could no longer nurse or take breast milk in bottles but instead were placed on formula mixed with rice cereal, thickened into almost smoothie consistency. The nurses assured me the twins had received the breast milk when it was most crucial, but it was still depressing. Aspiration could lead to pneumonia, though, and pneumonia would be devastating for a micropreemie so we began our new journey of trying to feed the babies the thickened formula.

Despite the change, the twins did well and hungrily took in their new bottles. The next thing we knew, they were finishing their feedings in ten to fifteen minutes which was a dramatic switch from the long and arduous process we had been pushing through before. While we praised our children for being thickened-liquid geniuses, someone noticed that the nipples the twins had been using had been cross-cut into an "X." While this used to be standard practice, it was firmly against current policy and the next thing we knew, hospital administrators were descending upon us to discuss the "cut nipple situation." It seemed like there was a fear of legal action, but that had never crossed our minds.

We were just disappointed that now that the problem was fixed and we had gone back to the regular nipples, the twins were once again unable to finish their bottles in the allotted thirty minutes. It was frustrating that after all each twin had overcome - ventilators, heart surgery, blood transfusions and test after test - we were stuck on something as basic as eating. Except, for a preemie, nothing is basic and in fact, eating takes much more work than most of us realize.

October 6th, my due date of 40 weeks and our goal date to have the twins home, came and went. We were so close, and the doctors decided it was time to move forward with our rooming in. This would involve us staying in a room at the end of the hall on the opposite side of the NICU doing everything on our own overnight with the nurse close within call. It had originally been scheduled over the weekend, but with the cut nipple incident, it got pushed forward to a weeknight which meant Brian would have to get up in the morning to go to work and I would be left alone with two oxygen-dependent newborns, mixing meds, making the formula with rice cereal, and trying to complete the feedings which were still a challenge. Thankfully, when we would go home from the hospital, Brian would be home with me for a week or two before I was on my own. We were both very nervous about rooming in on a weeknight, but there was nothing we could do to change it.

The night of the room-in, we each fed one twin the dinnertime bottle and the day nurse reviewed how to mix the medicines and formula. After the bottles, the room wasn't ready and probably wouldn't be for a bit so we dashed out for an hour, ducking into a local Chinese restaurant for some fuel before our first experience caring for two newborns overnight. We were both nervous and excited, rushing through our meals quickly to get back to the hospital. Shifts had changed which made everything feel a lot different. We knew the daytime staff so well it felt like one big family, but with the night shift, we almost felt new despite being on the unit well over a hundred days. Most of the nurses had cared for our babies and knew all about them and us, however we did not know many of them at all which made it feel fairly awkward. Close to 9:00 pm, the room was ready and the nurse, Brian, and I wheeled both babies and all of their equipment down the hall. For the walk, the twins used portable oxygen tanks, but when we reached the room, the tubing was not long enough to reach the oxygen outlet on the wall. We called in respiratory therapy and the therapist arrived, bringing some tubes and adapters to make things work, but he did not have the friendly demeanor of the daytime RT's we loved so much. The twins were fussing, hungry. This was not starting well.

The nurse and therapist left, and I began mixing powdered formula with water, rice cereal, and medicine at the tiny sink that resembled the one in my small college dorm room. I momentarily dreamt of our large countertop at home next to our kitchen sink with likely over ten times as much space and began to hope that if we could make it through it all in this setting, home might seem easier. Perhaps that was the plan.

We each held a baby and tried to feed them the bottles, but both only took part of the feeding. They would try to eat and then cry, try to eat and then cry. We tried holding, burping, swaddling, but to no avail. As it was a simulation of going home, they did not follow with tube feedings. Since we were tethered to the wall on such short makeshift oxygen tubes, we could barely stand with the twins, let along walk to soothe their hungry cries. We gave it our best effort at each feeding every three hours, but there was no improvement. Both twins were upset and crying, likely starving. Half-empty bottles and spilled powder formula littered every counter of the room. We finally gave up even turning off the lights to try to sleep; it was obvious something was going terribly wrong with the feedings and none of us were going to get any rest. The fact that this disaster had gotten shifted to a weeknight started to infuriate me.

Morning came and Brian had to get in the shower and prepare for work. By the time he left, I was trying unsuccessfully to feed Gavin and Hannah was hysterical. Because of my short leash of Gavin's oxygen to the wall, I couldn't even reach her. I set him down, tried to feed her, and he began to wail. I was in tears, alone with two screaming newborns who were both attached to the wall and with none of the help I would have at home. I gave in and called the nurse early. I could hardly speak. Thankfully, it was back to day shift and the nurse was one of our favorites. She was at our room within seconds, reswaddling babies, gently bouncing them, telling me all was fine and that we'd head back to our normal room. I managed to get out how they couldn't get enough to eat all night and how I knew they had to be hungry. Like magic, she managed to pack up our supplies and hook the twins to their portable oxygen tanks. I tried to reach out to push one of the beds, but she wouldn't allow it, saying I needed to rest, so I walked down the hall next to her with the bags as she pushed both babies back to their home base.

When we got back, she looked at the nipples we had been given for the bottles and told me to go home and sleep. I stopped for a coffee, completely distraught and utterly exhausted, and then headed home.

Later, they called to say the nipples were not the right ones, and that the holes were too small. The thickened formula would not come through the holes which led to two frustrated, hungry babies who were sucking on their bottles, but getting very little food. I would scream, too.

I was sent to the baby store to buy nipples that were two sizes larger that had much bigger openings for the thickened formula. Hannah and Gavin had full bellies once again, but it had been a nightmare I never wanted to repeat. We were all learning, the hospital included, with two micropreemies leading the way.

Chapter 22

Three weeks before the funneling diagnosis

THE WIND WHIPPED MY HAIR AROUND and I breathed in the fresh scent of saltwater. I was standing in a field of purple flowers near San Francisco. Brian and I had been driving the Pacific Coast Highway with his parents beginning in San Diego and traveling up to this point, taking in sights along the way. We had watched sea lions in La Jolla, spent the night in Morro Bay, enjoyed fresh seafood, toured a castle, and shopped in Chinatown. I was eighteen weeks pregnant and after being so afraid to announce our pregnancy due to the trials of our infertility, we were finally comfortable making it known. I had been surprised in California that when I put on my summer dresses, I had a small baby bump beginning to show.

I looked back at Brian who held up his phone. I turned sideways so the small bump could be seen against the ocean as the flowers danced in the wind around my ankles. We were so happy. I smiled as he took what would be one of the last photos we would have showing my pregnancy with our twins.

Chapter 23

With everything finally settled with the thickened formula and the appropriate nipples, both twins were finally able to take to eating and discussions of discharge resumed. After nearly four months in the NICU, during which time it had often seemed like "home" was an abstract concept too far away to even imagine, suddenly we were frantic to get everything finished in time. Both twins would go home on oxygen and apnea monitors which are machines that sound an alarm if the baby stops breathing. We had a representative come to the NICU to train us on the use of portable oxygen tanks and another come to our house to bring us a concentrator and a few large, missile-like tanks that were stored in our garage in case of a power outage. Our front door now displayed a bright "oxygen in use" sign to alert firefighters in case of an emergency.

Appointments were arranged. The first week home, we would take trips to the pediatrician, cardiologist, and liver specialist. Within a few weeks, we would add a visit to the retina specialist and representatives from the in-home therapy service would come see us to evaluate and begin therapy. All the while, a home health nurse would visit twice a week to measure weight gain and assess for complications.

The hospital created a folder with each baby's medical conditions and medications for us, for their doctors, and in case of emergency. Prescriptions were filled, and the local compounding pharmacy came to know me by name. My official twelve weeks of full-time maternity leave began.

Amidst the preparation for discharge, our babies continued to hit milestones. They both passed their carseat tests, sitting upright strapped into their carseats for over an hour with no drops in oxygen or heart rate. They aced the newborn hearing screens and received their second round of vaccines. Gavin was circumcised. Brian and I had gotten the required flu and Tdap shots in September, but now our parents got theirs since it had to be done before they could visit our home. We stocked up on sanitizer and diapers.

Hannah and Gavin were perfect. They were now over seven pounds. Hannah was doing so well, the doctors even trialed her off oxygen completely, but it left her exhausted so it was decided not to push it and that she would go home on oxygen after all. There were tiny reminders on their bodies of the battles they had valiantly fought. Gavin had a jagged, horizontal scar on his back from the heart surgery and one right beneath it from his chest tube. He also had an electrode-shaped scar on his abdomen from when his micropreemie skin was so thin, a simple lead attached to a wire left a scar when it was removed. Hannah had multiple scars on her ankles from all of the IV's. I knew I would teach them about each of these marks and describe how brave they had been, even at just one pound. I already hoped that knowing their story would help them believe in themselves in the future and would give them confidence, faith, and bravery when times became hard.

A tentative discharge date was set. Our friends took us out to dinner at a beautiful, lakefront seafood restaurant for one last "date night" as we would be on lockdown once the twins came home, unable to leave the house with them except for doctor's appointments. We would have no baby-sitters for a year or two due to the medical issues, oxygen, and monitors. We spent most of the evening talking about the kids, marveling at how far they had come and all of the odds they had beaten.

On October 16th, 2013, after 122 days in the NICU and one day shy of Hannah and Gavin's four month birthday, it was time to go home. I had barely scrubbed into the unit before nurses, therapists, and doctors began coming up to me, offering smiles and congratulations. I handed my preemie book back to the social worker. There were tears in my eyes before I even passed the charge nurse's desk. This team was now part of our family. They had saved the lives of our babies too many times to count. They had endured the tough times right there with us, had laughed and joked with us, had offered hugs when needed and given space when they could sense that would be best. This was not just a job for all of these incredible individuals, but instead, a calling to which they were dedicating their lives. You can never thank someone enough for giving you the most tremendous gift there is, that of loving your child as if he or she were their own.

Our nurse for discharge day was Andrea, who had teenage twins of her own. She was spunky and always full of energy which I realized was good when I saw how much work was involved in sending two kids home a third of a year after they had been admitted to intensive care. She explained the hospital could not reuse anything that had been opened so I filled bags with diapers, wipes, thermometers, creams, and anything else we had used in the drawers. It was astonishing how much accumulated in four months. By the time Brian arrived after work, I'd already made multiple trips to my car, filling it with supplies, the twins' clean and dirty clothes, stuffed animals, banners, blood pressure cuffs, and footprint cards. I wanted to save every memory. I even stripped the calendars from the wall outlining weekly expectations and goals.

Andrea ended up staying an hour past the end of her twelve-hour shift to finish up all of our paperwork and help us prepare for the big departure. Meanwhile, we made sure Hannah and Gavin were clean, dressed, diapered, and in hats before transferring them to their carseats and hooking them to their portable oxygen tanks. Their apnea monitors were switched on to watch their breathing and heart rate the way we would at home. For the first time since the twins had so urgently entered the world 122 days earlier, the monitors in the room were switched off, dark and silent. The black screens were unnerving. You couldn't help but imagine other ways it all could have gone, other micropreemie situations when those same monitors had been shut down.

Hannah and Gavin slept in their carseats as we signed form after form. It was exciting, but also terrifying. Were we really ready to be on our own with these fragile, oxygen-dependent babies? I was thankful we would be leaving during night shift. We had become so close with everyone on day shift that I knew I would have completely broken down leaving all of the familiar faces who had done so much for our children. Everyone on night shift had done just as much and I appreciated them equally, but due to the times we visited, I didn't have the chance to know many of them as well.

It was time.

Our NICU room was empty except for two babies dozing in carseats and two empty beds. Housekeeping staff was hovering, preparing to deep clean our room for the next set of twins. Due to hospital policy, we could not carry our twins to the car so Andrea picked up a carseat in each hand while Brian and I carried the tanks and monitors, and we all headed down the hall. I was wearing the same flannel shirt I had tucked the twins beneath again and again while doing kangaroo care holds the first couple months. We paused for a photo as we left and nurses who happened to be in the main hall wished us well with big smiles. We left the unit with Andrea carrying our miracles, rode the elevator downstairs, and walked to the hospital door where Brian went to retrieve my car. We placed the carseats into their bases and rechecked the straps. Oxygen tanks and apnea monitors were tucked securely onto the floor and then finally, it was really and truly time. We hugged Andrea and I got into the driver's seat. While Brian got his car, I was almost panicked with fear at the idea of driving home on the highway with such precious cargo in the backseat. My radio was off; I wanted no distractions. It was the first moment of the rest of our journey, and we were now solely responsible for keeping our children safe.

We pulled away from the hospital one final time. It was dark outside as we left the parking lot, but as I looked back at the towering building that had been the twins' home for their first four months, lights were on in many of the rooms including those on the fourth floor in the NICU. Their work would continue. More babies would burst forth into the world, too early and too small, and these amazing individuals would continue to work day and night, saving these tiny lives. It was a place of miracles, of faith, of hope, and most of all, a place of overwhelming, never-failing, self-sacrificing love.

We merged onto the highway, finally going home.

• Part 2 – Home •

Chapter 24

OUR FIRST NIGHT AT HOME WAS A COMPLETE DISASTER. Brian and I huddled in the nursery, each trying to feed a baby the formula (now store-bought as opposed to hospital-issued) that we had mixed with rice cereal exactly according to our instructions and once again, feeding dysfunction won the battle. This time, despite triple-checking our instructions, the liquid inside the bottles was too thin so instead of starving, our babies were now choking. We added more and more rice cereal, trying to achieve the same consistency we had at the hospital, but it was impossible to get it right without having a correct formula. We managed to get it thick enough that the twins could eat some, but they were still hungry and unhappy. I made it only a few hours before I called the NICU, but nothing could be done until the speech therapist arrived at 8:00 the next day. In addition, we started to notice that the steady sheen of sweat building up on our backs and foreheads might be from more than stress; the oxygen concentrator in the twins' room was slowly raising the temperature until it was nearly unbearable. We opened a window and turned the ceiling fan on high to get some cool October air, but the temperature continued to rise. By morning, we called the oxygen company who reassured us that a little rise in temperature was normal. At this point, the twins' room was well over 80 degrees and there was nothing to do but clear a spot in the spare room and drag the concentrator inside. The oxygen tube now ran from the spare room into the hall and then beneath the nursery door where it continued up to the twins. Our cat promptly began gnawing on the cord in the hall. The twins immediately yanked their tubing off as it was no longer held to their cheeks by the firm, circular hospital stickers but instead by tiny pieces of cheap adhesive provided by the oxygen company. Within a day, their cheeks were pink from continually pulling off the stickers and their nasal cannulas were usually hanging down around their mouths as opposed to in their nostrils.

Our first full day home, amidst the oxygen and feeding crises, a man arrived at our house to change our TV service to a satellite company. Brian had found us a great deal where we could now have movie channels and libraries of other movies available so I would have a lot to watch when I was home with the kids. This was all great, but with two micropreemies, we wanted zero germ exposure so the twins and I remained isolated in the sweltering nursery while the installation was in process. They were crying, still hungry from lack of food, and Brian had to stay with the workman downstairs. It took hours and all three of us were miserable. The door finally opened and when I looked up, expecting Brian, one of our friends had stopped by to check in. At first I was embarrassed we were failing so miserably on just the first day, but having two girls herself, she immediately began to help and assured me it was normal to feel this way.

"It's okay to curse. They can't talk yet."

She reminded me that it was okay to feel stressed with a newborn. Not just that, I had two newborns plus a mess of medical equipment to figure out. With her help, I was able to wipe away the tears, take a few deep breaths, and give the day a new start. The installation was eventually finished and Brian could return to help. We could finally leave the nursery and move downstairs where there was more room and fresh air. The speech therapist called us back. She had gone to the store and worked with store-bought formula and rice until she had a good recipe for us and once we mixed this up, the twins were once again able to eat and the crying eased. Brian and I moved as a team taking turns mixing formula, adding medication, and washing bottles while both feeding babies every three hours. It took the twins nearly an hour to finish a bottle and often, the grand finale was suddenly vomiting back up all of what they had painstakingly consumed.

The next day, the twins had their first appointment with the pediatrician. It was the first time we packed up both babies, both oxygen tanks, and both apnea monitors, loaded the kids into their carseats and then into the double stroller. The doctor added another medication for reflux but otherwise gave a good report. Also in the first week, the home health nurse began to visit, bringing a baby scale. Both twins had lost weight since being at home, and the formula had to be altered once again to add more calories. We continued our routine of documenting every diaper and temperature reading every three hours along with how much each baby ate at each feeding. Initially, Brian and I both woke every three hours to feed a baby for an hour, but we quickly learned it was better for each of us to take a solo shift, feeding both babies for up to two hours, and then letting the other parent catch the next shift. We drove downtown for Hannah to see the liver specialist who gave her the all-clear from her cholestatic jaundice. Next it was on to the cardiologist and after Hannah wailed through an echocardiogram, the doctor pronounced her heart condition stable and decided to see her again in a few months to recheck. For each appointment, we had to carefully count backwards and plan. It took close to an hour to drive to each appointment, fifteen minutes to load the car, the twins both needed a bottle right before we left (which would take an hour) and then if we weren't home from the appointment within another hour, the next bottle would be late, throwing off the entire schedule.

Brian had to go back to work after a week and a half. The day he went back to work, the twins had a check with the retina specialist so I recruited my mom to come with us to help. This was going to be a long appointment so I had to pack everything necessary to mix the bottles – water, rice, formula, medication, and measuring spoons. Then we packed up both kids, the oxygen tanks, and the monitors and began the forty-minute drive to the office.

We were driving through one of the busiest highway interchanges in the city when in the back seat, an apnea monitor began to sound. Typically, when the monitors had alarmed thus far, it was just a couple alerts that stopped quickly when the babies were able to regulate their breathing or heart rate. My mom twisted around and told me it was Gavin as she shook the edge of the carseat. It wasn't uncommon for the alarms to sound if the twins were sleeping too deeply, causing their breathing to slow and heart rate to fall. In those cases, gently waking them regulated their breathing. This time, however, the shaking did nothing. The alarm continued as I pulled the car over on the edge of the highway as cars flew around us at over seventy miles per hour. It was likely one of the worst places in the city to pull over, but when your child isn't breathing, there is no other option. I could do nothing but pray other drivers were paying attention and that I had pulled over far enough as I leapt out of the car and yanked open the back door. Gavin was asleep and as I rubbed his chest, his eyes opened and the alarm stopped. We will never know if it was a legitimate alarm or if the monitor was not reading quite right from the band around his chest, but as he gazed up at me through sleepy eyes, I could breathe again.

We made it to the retina specialist's office so they could complete yet another eye exam. The twins screamed as the skin around their eyes was held back with clamps and their eyes were dilated and examined. I tried to mix formula and spilled an entire container all over the carpet. The doctor cleared both twins of retinopathy of prematurity and I was so thankful, not only because we had avoided a major medical issue but also because I felt the entire visit had been a disaster I never wanted to attempt again. We stopped to feed the twins in the lobby on the way out, and one threw up, our cue to bid our final farewell to the retina clinic.

I learned to take care of both twins by myself. Brian began making large jugs of formula and water so I only had to add the rice and medication before warming it, taking less time. Each morning, when the twins were up for the day, I would dress them and we would lay on the soft giraffe rug in their room as they cooed and moved around, taking in the animals and trees on their walls, their mommy and each other. I would then carry them each downstairs using extra- long tubing that ran from the concentrator in the spare room to the family room. We continued to battle our cat chewing through the line and we finally convinced the oxygen company to let us use small, portable tanks during the day which meant less tubing to control. This required them to come by our house every week or so, retrieving empty tanks and bringing us new ones, which they made clear was not the way they preferred, but with two newborn, oxygen-dependent micropreemies to care for by myself all day, I couldn't bring myself to care.

Once we were downstairs and the twins were attached to their portable tanks, we began the feeding process which then essentially took the rest of our day. I sat cross-legged on the floor cradling one baby in my lap, feeding the formula/rice smoothie, with the other baby nestled on a pillow, often sleeping. After about an hour, I switched to feeding the second baby. Which baby was fed first was simple – whoever acted hungrier. Besides the pillow, I used a baby swing and bouncy seats to entertain one while feeding the other and when we were finished, I would often lay them both on their ocean play mat. They gazed up at whales and starfish as I read to them, brought them toys, sang songs, and played with their tiny feet. I rolled them onto their bellies for tummy time as I lay in front of them, making funny faces or placing musical toys within their sight. Each night, we were allowed to take off the apnea monitors for a few minutes as I bathed them, but the oxygen tubing remained. Once they had dried, the monitors were wrapped back around their chests and plugged back in. To carry a baby anywhere, you had a three-foot oxygen tank and a monitor the size of a laptop both slung over your shoulder. It was impossible to carry both babies at one time.

We began to adjust to our routine at home. On the good days, you felt like a super parent. We were caring for not just one baby, but two. In addition to being their parents, we were their nurses, therapists, advocates, and teachers. We managed the equipment and became experts at mixing medications and formula. On the bad days, we took it a minute at a time and watched the calendar for the next appointment; every follow-up was one step closer to getting rid of some of the wires and tubes.

Halloween arrived two weeks after our return home. I placed the Little Red Riding Hood and wolf crocheted hats on the kids and laid them on a blanket as they slept through my amateur photo shoot. For the first time in years, we kept our door closed and our lights off to deter trick-or-treaters. In years past, Brian had dressed up in extravagant outfits and wigs, entertaining the neighborhood kids with chain saw escapades, black lights, and scary music; this year, each trick-or-treater was viewed as a host of germs and I wanted them nowhere near our front door.

By November, Hannah, who had developed into a little chunk with rolls on her arms and legs, had begun to offer up some smiles. We returned for a NICU follow-up appointment and she did well enough on her oxygen tests that she was released from the oxygen during the day, continuing to wear it at night. The monitor remained on throughout the entire day. Gavin still needed oxygen, but his was turned down to almost as low as it could go. The doctor rolled her eyes at the fact that the oxygen company continued to refuse to provide us with good stickers for their faces and she dug through their drawers, giving us all she could find. Simply being able to use proper stickers on the twins' cheeks that actually held their oxygen in place without constantly ripping their skin lowered our overall stress level dramatically.

When it came time for Thanksgiving, we declined our invitation to the traditional large family gathering as we would continue to be on lockdown, only leaving for doctor appointments, for many more months. My parents came over and we had a quiet Thanksgiving at home. We had Amy, our photographer, come to our house for a "newborn" photo shoot, despite the fact that the twins were nearly five months old.

December arrived and I barely registered the drop in temperature or occasional snowfall since I rarely left the house. Gavin began to smile as well; the first time he smiled, he was enjoying a ride on the baby swing in cowboy pajamas right after his bath, and his whole face lit up as he looked at me. This baby was *happy*; every chest compression, every needle stick, every blood transfusion was worth it because here he was, no longer trapped in an isolette enduring constant medical interventions, but just an actual happy child. We returned to the hospital for a second NICU follow-up and Gavin was released from oxygen during the day as well. It was a new thrill to be able to pick up a baby and simply swing the apnea monitor over my shoulder. Our babies were so *portable*.

Portable only around the house, of course. There would be no pictures of a tiny baby on Santa's lap; I could practically see the germs crawling on the suits of the Santas at the stores and it made me shudder. Once again, we stayed away from the large family gathering for Christmas and settled for nice celebrations at home with our parents. For the most part, we felt like the twins were now huge however they were still dwarfed by a Christmas stocking. The twins both loved to stare up at the twinkling lights on the Christmas tree, and I would play

Christmas music throughout the day which always made them kick and smile. We happily hung "Our First Christmas" ornaments on the tree and posed the kids in front, wearing their holiday attire. We were so happy to be home, and my heart ached for the babies and their families who were celebrating such a special day in intensive care.

While doing the stretches our hospital therapist had taught me, I began to notice a difference in how Hannah and Gavin's legs felt. While Hannah was loose and limber, Gavin was developing tension. I had to convince his taut muscles to give enough for me to straighten his knee and raise his leg up away from the ground. When lying on their backs, Hannah's feet relaxed but Gavin's pointed down practically straight. I immediately pushed for a physical therapy consult. The physical therapist assessed both twins and decided Gavin needed physical therapy at least several times a month. It was far too early to determine, likely over a year too early, but feeling how his muscles felt beneath my hands, I knew that Gavin likely had cerebral palsy. We knew of the high risk from his grade four brain hemorrhage. With his increased muscle tone and his medical history, the chance of it being anything else was next to zero. No one, not the pediatrician or the physical therapist, was going to come out and say this is what they suspected, but I had enough experience to know the suspicions inside their heads. I didn't even tell Brian exactly what I knew; I only explained what we were feeling in his muscles and the ways we could stretch him to help. I knew Brian well enough to know that he would tell me it was too early and I was worrying about something that had not been diagnosed. People with cerebral palsy present with a vast range of ability, and Gavin had shown other good signs like tracking well with his eyes and grasping a rattle, so

I stayed positive although I began to accept what I knew was the eventual inevitable diagnosis.

I returned to work two days a week and my mom arrived on those days to care for the twins. We taught her CPR and how to manage the monitors. She learned to mix the medication I had described on a list on our refrigerator. Each night, I prepped clothes and diapers. I mixed a large jug of formula and water, laying out the rice cereal and measuring equipment. On my first day back, my boss had a bouquet of flowers and a coffee on my desk. I made it less than thirty minutes before I texted home, finding out they were all fine, of course. My mom began to fall into a routine as well, managing the hour-long feedings and running the monitors with ease. It was equal parts terrifying and satisfying to be away and have some time with adults however I found that I spent most of the days discussing my kids with my patients as they all wanted to hear the story. I loved my job, but I could hardly wait to be home each night since I missed the twins so much.

We moved into a new year, and the twins continued to make astonishing progress. They were released from oxygen all together and then their apnea monitors as well. For over six months, every breath had been continually monitored and for the first time, we laid them in their cribs at night without the comfort of knowing we would be alerted if they stopped breathing. I checked continuously, watching the gentle rise and fall of their chests and at some point, I fell into a fitful sleep. Yet there they were in the morning, unmonitored, breathing and ready to be fed. Without the monitors, we could at last simply pick up our babies. We could hold them, rock them, lay them down, sit them in their baby seats, and carry them around the house without even a strap over our shoulders. Our movements felt almost like floating, they were so free. The oxygen company arrived to load up the concentrator, the large extra tanks in our garage, and all remaining portable tanks. We wrapped up the tubing and cheek stickers, stashing them away in drawers just in case but also very much out of sight, hoping to never see them again.

Winter began to thaw into spring. Gavin was fitted for a cranial helmet to resolve the large flat spot on his head that had developed because he continuously looked to the right. We stretched and positioned him as best we could, but his high muscle tone contributed to keeping his neck muscles taut. I placed toys and books on his left side and over time, he became more and more willing to turn and stretch his neck. The smiles abounded and giggles erupted. We couldn't go outside so we dressed up in our fuzzy winter coats and gigantic snowsuits in the living room, and I took pictures as they grinned up at me out of the fleece. They struggled with eating rice cereal on a spoon so an occupational therapist was brought onto our team to help them eat without gagging or choking.

Hannah rolled over and a few months later, her brother did as well. We battled our first bout of illness when the twins were diagnosed with RSV. Thankfully, with the RSV antibody shots they received each month the first winter ($2,000 per kid per shot, mercifully covered by insurance for approved children), they made it through with barely a scratch and no need to return to oxygen. I began to take them on walks in the neighborhood, our first venture out of the house yet still far away from people and their germs. I hung signs on their carseats and stroller asking people not to touch them however I learned people inevitably want to grab at babies' hands and feet. The first time a neighbor came up to us and touched them, I had to practically hold myself back from yanking her well-meaning arm away and when she wasn't looking, I doused the babies with the sanitizer I continually carried with me.

Each year, the local children's hospital uses data based on local and nationwide reports of flu and RSV to determine when patients would be most at risk for contracting one of these dangerous illnesses. They recommend minimizing exposure and during this time, families with micropreemies and medically fragile children often hunker down as much as possible, staying on lockdown and only leaving the house when absolutely required. The year the twins were born, lockdown began in September (while we were still in the hospital) and was finally lifted in early April. We decided our first official outing would be to my extended family's celebration of Easter. Everyone in the family knew of the dangers of illness, and we were certain no one would be there who had even the slightest hint of being sick. We brought sanitizer but when we arrived, my mom had already placed large tubs of it in each room. We carried the twins around as they "hunted" for eggs and by the time we reached Easter baskets, Gavin was fast asleep in Brian's arms. Hannah hungrily reached for every toy and book, wanting each of them on her lap until only her eyes could be seen peering out among the gifts. Before we left, we placed the twins next to their second cousin, Asher, for pictures and it was the first time they had been anywhere near another child. Children were the most terrifying of all when it came to germs. At this point, I pictured kids as small, loveable petri dishes. For several days after we returned home, I held my breath waiting for certain illness to arrive, but we eventually realized we had made it through and they were not getting sick.

A year passed. Hannah and Gavin celebrated their first birthday. We met our photographer once again. The twins sprawled on the grass in their onesies marked with "1," holding frames that held their first pictures when they were just a pound and ventilator-dependent, barely resembling babies at all. We planned a celebration for all of our family, and I strung onesies on clotheslines ranging from preemie size to the 12-month clothes they wore on that day. The preemie onesies that had swallowed them up at 2 months now seemed impossibly small. Could they have ever really been that size? Had it all been real?

As our family showered the twins with love and gifts, it was all talk of what an adventure it had been. There were tears and laughter. We placed birthday hats on the twins' heads and the children who had not yet been able to handle solid food tore into birthday cake with a vengeance. We laughed as they shoveled it into their mouths, their chubby faces and bodies sticky with cake crumbs and frosting. Yes, it had been a harrowing journey, but it had also been a wonderful one and in that moment, they were simply two happy one-year-olds discovering cake for the first time, surrounded by people who loved them.

We were not naïve to the long road that lay ahead. When they turned one, the twins were not yet crawling and Gavin was not yet sitting, but we hoped in time they would. And, eventually, they did. We ignored timelines and simply set goals which both twins continued to meet in their own time. Hannah learned to pull herself up and began to take unsteady, toddler steps. Gavin was fitted with ankle braces as soon as he first managed to pull up. He progressed from a stander to a gait trainer to a walker and eventually to independent steps, tottering from his physical therapist to me at 22 months old.

People tell you things later that they don't tell you in the beginning. Our pediatrician told us he never imagined our twins would look as good as they did on their first visit when he read their history; he had been expecting the worst. One of our therapy coordinators raved about how well they were doing; after all, they were *twenty-four weekers*. Gavin was almost three years old before his physical therapist told me he was the highest functioning kid she has seen with a grade four brain hemorrhage.

We had been through almost the worst, but we were also living the best. Life could not and would not ever be the same. Issues that had seemed big before were insignificant after watching our newborn children fight for their lives. We were beyond lucky, we were blessed. Our children lived because of the gifted touch of so many individuals, because we happen to live in a society with advanced medical care, because people are out there day after day researching and innovating new medical advances and, quite simply, because God granted us a miracle.

• Part 3 – Free •

Chapter 25

TODAY, HANNAH AND GAVIN ARE THREE YEARS OLD. If you ask them, they are "free" – just like almost any other three-year-old would tell you. And free they are – free of oxygen, free of monitors, free of restrictions carried by liver and heart conditions. Free to run and play and learn like any other child.

Gavin is sweet and sensitive while also being equally mischievous and inquisitive. His smile stills my heart. He loves cars, trucks, and diggers. He would live outside if we'd allow it with his bubble mower and sticks he uses as weed-eaters and leaf blowers, doing everything he can to be just like his daddy. He carries a pint-sized drill around the house fixing furniture and trucks, but it's not uncommon to see him stop to feed one of Hannah's baby dolls a bottle or listen to a stuffed animal with a stethoscope. He wears sunglasses to read books and informs us they are "reading glasses" just like his preschool teacher's. He is our snuggler and our questioner that never lets anything slip by him. He informs me, "I was tiny when I was born."

Gavin has been officially diagnosed with spastic diplegia cerebral palsy, the result of his grade four brain hemorrhage. It causes him to have high muscle tone in both of his legs although the right is worse than the left and his arms are mildly affected as well. When he learned to stand and walk, he rose up onto his toes developing blisters and callouses on the tips, but his physical therapist got him into ankle braces immediately to correct his position as much as possible. Now, despite his diagnosis, he walks and runs with and without his ankle braces (he picked out his most recent pair, a car and truck design, of course). He falls a fair amount, but he has learned how to stand up and by the time he announces "I'm okay," he is often already moving on to his next adventure. He runs, he swims, and he scales the rock wall on the swing set. He had physical, occupational, and speech therapists come to our home for three years, and he is now receiving therapy through the school district as well as a private clinic. He absolutely loves therapy. He crawls through tunnels, plays in sand boxes, walks on balance beams, makes crafts using scissors, and plays with every imaginable type of ball. There will always be obstacles. He may soon receive his first round of injections into his arms, legs, and trunk to decrease the tension in his muscles. He has never exceeded the first percentile in height or weight although our pediatrician is not concerned about his size, focusing instead on his overall astounding development. When the twins began preschool, they were swept under by the germs they had never been exposed to and with Gavin's lungs, he was in and out of various emergency rooms for months with croup and asthma attacks. We added a pulmonologist, ENT, and an asthma specialist to our team and with new medication and time, he is improving every day. He has worked so hard to gain so much independence and when he proclaims he wants to do things himself, I smile with a mix of pride and sadness, like any other parent.

Hannah is our tiny princess. She has brown hair like her daddy and is usually sporting a large, bright bow of her choice. She is our firecracker. She sings, she dances, and outside, she simply loves to run. She begs us to chase her as she sprints around the swing set, races through the leaves, and takes off toward the fence to love on the neighbor's dog. She started dance class, and despite the fact that she is the tiniest dancer in the class of twenty girls, she taps and plies right along in the front row. She adores animals, accessories, stuffed toys, and giving kisses. She calls her brother "G-bug," and grabs his hand, pulling him around our house. She can scale the ladder on our full-size swing set like a ten-year-old and sends herself soaring down the slide without any help. She sneaks up on our cats, hugging them like teddy bears.

Hannah had speech and occupational therapy in our home until she turned three and then when tested, her scores showed she had caught up to her peers and no additional services were required. She has been fully cleared by the liver specialist with no residual problems. She is doing so well with her heart condition that her cardiologist has now extended her check-ups to once every two to three years. At this point, he is fairly certain her heart condition won't affect her life at all. After being born at 24 weeks and just a bit over one pound, she now appears to be entirely caught up with other children her age. Other than being small, the only evidence she has of being a micropreemie is the presence of tiny scars on her ankles from all of the needle sticks.

Brian and I had only been married four years when the twins made their dramatic entrance into the world, crash landing into the NICU where they had to fight valiantly for so long. I heard stories of marriages that fell apart following significant NICU stays, and I've read the controversial statistic that up to 80% of marriages involving children with special needs end in divorce. I believe marriages in these situations have to move strongly in one direction or the other. Either two people are able to band together and fight alongside one another, holding each other up when one is too weak to stand... or everything collapses. With a child in intensive care, there is no way a marriage can remain the way it was before. I know our marriage is different now than it was before the NICU, but we were able to stand side-by-side, united in our unshakeable love for these two children and each other, with a common goal of refusing to lose hope despite how dismal the situation became. After facing adversity, fear, and tragedy, but also love, hope, and faith, I believe our marriage is stronger now that it was before the arrival of the twins.

Our lives will never be the same as they would have been if the twins had been born closer to term. With every cold they get, we hold our breath and wait for the signs of respiratory distress that we know lead to a trip to the emergency room. We keep a seal-shaped nebulizer in the closet to use for breathing treatments for asthma and croup. We will continue to fill our days with therapy appointments and physician visits, and I have to constantly remind myself that I cannot shield them from everything bad in the world. At times, I feel myself become bitter when someone tells me they understand what we went through because they had a preemie, too, born at 35 weeks. I feel my heart start to harden because how could they possibly understand without the vents, without the brain hemorrhages, without having to watch their baby gasp and struggle to breathe for months, but then I remind myself that every baby's story is unique and having a premature baby born at any age is always terrifying to a new parent. I have since met mothers of babies born full-term who suffered through their own different, life-threatening journeys. Warriors in the NICU come in all shapes and sizes, each of them with their own miraculous tale to tell.

We will never know why our pregnancy ended so abruptly the way it did. There are theories. Perhaps it was due to twin pregnancy alone although multiples are born every day without this complication. Maybe there had been an undiagnosed trauma during a routine Pap test in my past. Would knowing matter, though? If we could change it all, would we? Obviously, you never want your children to have to suffer through pain and if I could take away the struggles Gavin will likely face with his CP, I would, but we are all products of the paths we have walked. Brian, Hannah, Gavin, and I are who we are today because of the way their story began. Our lives have been punctuated by people we never would have met. We met nurses who left their families for twelve-hour shifts while they stood guard over our children instead, continually adjusting ventilator settings so our babies could simply breathe. We have therapists who are so much like family that Gavin asks to see them every day. We have watched Hannah develop into a girl who strives to help others which I feel developed from clapping and cheering for her brother to meet milestones for years. We have seen Gavin develop into a three-year-old who is abnormally sensitive to the way other people are feeling. He is willing to snuggle just a little more than the average preschooler because the physical work of play, for him, can sometimes be a bit hard. Perhaps these would have been their personalities anyway, but to me, it seems impossible that they have not been shaped by it all; yes, some of it bad but much of it astoundingly good.

Three years later, our hospital NICU now attempts to intubate micropreemies born at 22 weeks. Recently, there was a little girl born there at 22 weeks, 5 days which was my gestation when I was admitted to the hospital, knowing if I delivered that night, there was nothing that could be done. The little girl took weeks to reach the 1 pound 9 ounce weight of our children, but she eventually did and while her future is as uncertain as all of ours, she lived and she has a chance. Every single night of my life, when I lie in bed and prepare to sleep, I remember. I remember the fear, I remember the heartbreak, but I never feel sad. I feel impossibly happy.

Looking back, I can still see the tiny forms in the glass isolettes on the edge of viability. I will never forget the needles, the wires, the tubes, and how hard they had to fight to simply breathe. Some may ask if it was all worth it. Should that much effort be put into saving a life that fragile, a life that should not even exist?

You tell me.

Watch Gavin's face light up as he soars through the air on his swing, with his eyes hidden behind his favorite red sunglasses but his face shining in a smile, as he asks Mommy to sing "Row, Row, Row Your Boat." Watch Hannah as she gallops around the yard riding an imaginary pony exclaiming "Hee Haw!" before she sprints off to kick a ball or create a masterpiece with sidewalk chalk. Listen as they say "I love you *so* much" and watch as they race around the house, holding hands, with their laughter ringing out above the music playing their favorite songs.

I wouldn't change a day.

It is now time to give back. We bring gifts to the NICU; tiny sleeper pajamas and blankets that feel like clouds. Every time we arrive, we walk the same route Brian and I took for 122 days. Although the hospital has upgraded and likely looks different to most people, it will always be the same for me. My heart beats quickly as I make my way to the elevator and I have to pause a minute when the doors open, revealing the lobby full of anxious NICU family members and the steady hum of the NICU staff running about completing their jobs. It almost makes me want to run away, but then I look down and see two curious faces looking back up at me, one with a mop of yellow blonde hair and another with brown pigtails, each with their fingers curled around a bag of gifts that they know are for tiny babies and everything is good and exactly as it should be. Our obstacles are large, but our team is strong.

I would do it all again, a hundred times over, to live just one more day of this life. Tomorrow, as two small hands reach out for mine, I will take them and follow where they lead.

Just as we did three years ago.

Hannah's first photo – June 17, 2013 – 24 weeks, 1 day

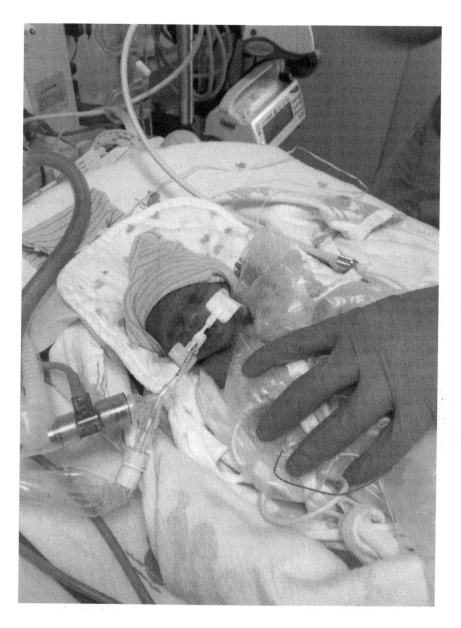

Gavin's first photo – June 17, 2013 – 24 weeks, 1 day

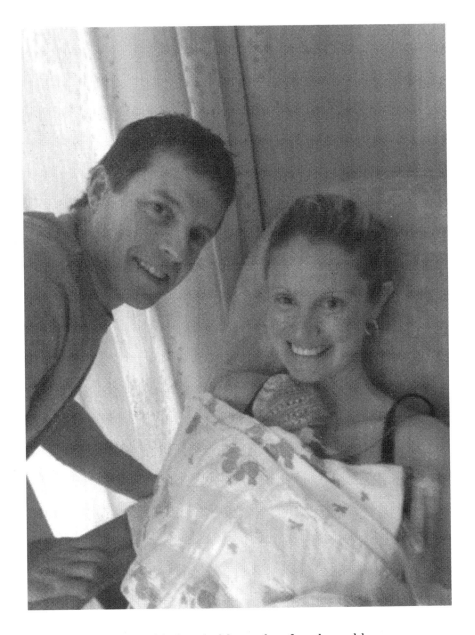

Hannah's first hold at only a few days old

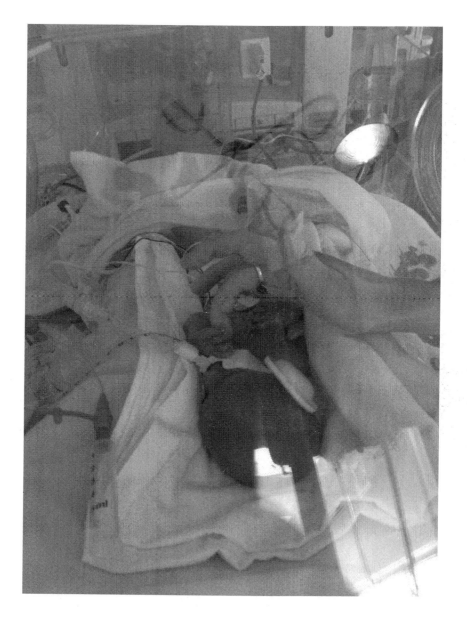

Gavin with his yellow oscillator "earmuff"

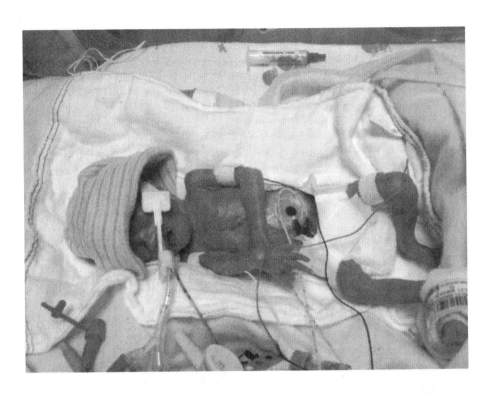

Hannah at a few days old, eyes still fused shut

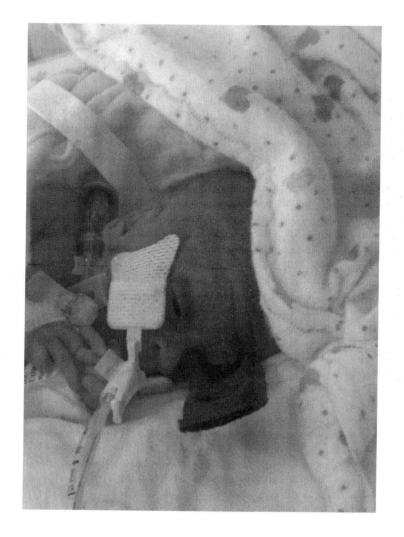

Gavin, trying to open an eye

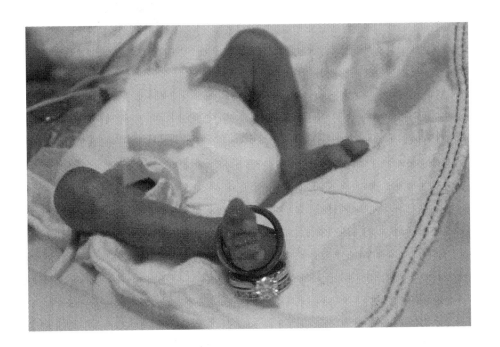

Hannah's tiny foot inside Daddy's ring

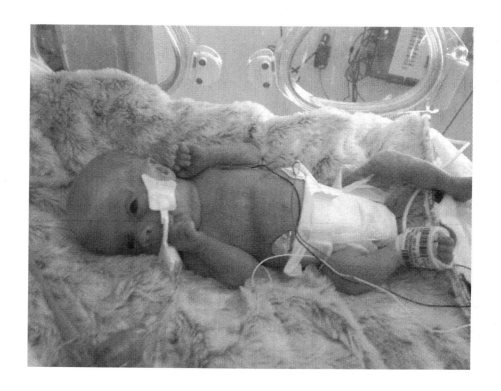

Gavin, alert and getting stronger

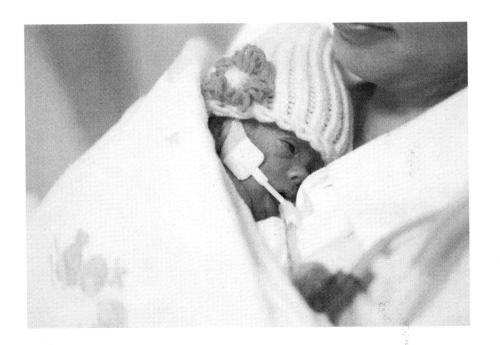

Kangaroo care with Hannah at 7 weeks

Photo by Amy Kuntz

Gavin, at 7 weeks, being transferred to kangaroo care

Photo by Amy Kuntz

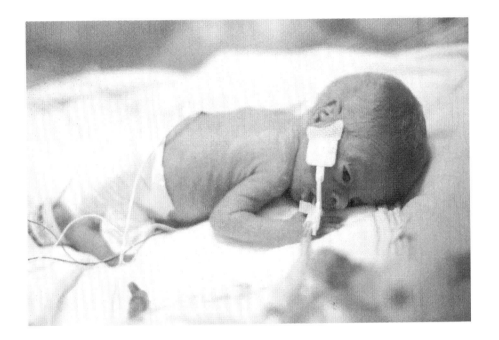

Gavin, 7 weeks

Photo by Amy Kuntz

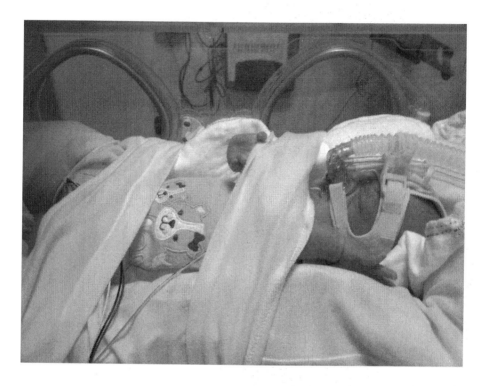

Hannah, on CPAP, wearing clothes for the first time

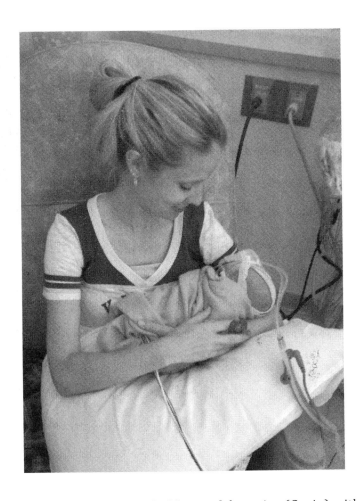

The first time I was able to hold one of the twins (Gavin) without kangaroo care

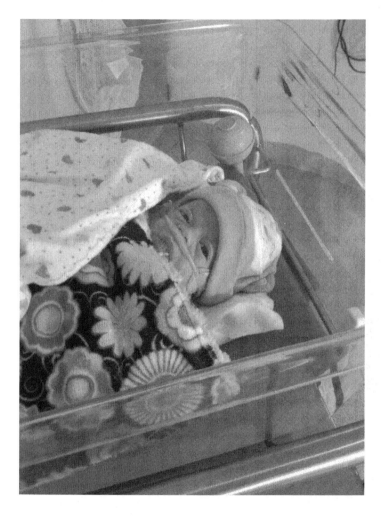

Hannah – on high-flow nasal cannula

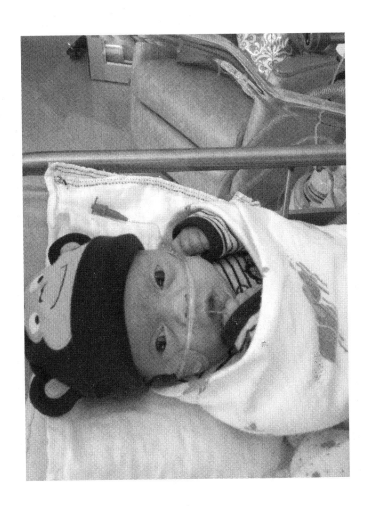

Gavin – on nasal cannula

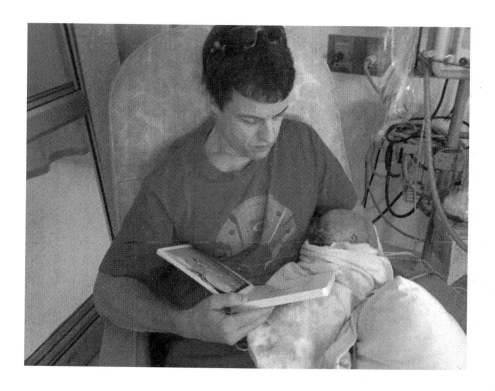

Brian, reading to Gavin

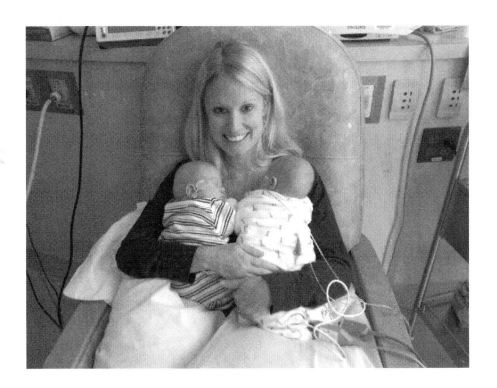

Twins back together for the first time in three months

Halloween 2013 – 4 months old – at home!

Our "newborn shoot" at home November 2013

Twins were 5 months old

Photo by Amy Kuntz

5 months

Photo by Amy Kuntz

9 months

One year old

Photo by Amy Kuntz

Gavin gets his first set of AFO's (ankle braces) at 16 months

Hannah, age 2

Photo by Amy Kuntz

Gavin, age 2

Photo by Amy Kuntz

Our family 2015

Photo by Amy Kuntz

Hannah, age 3

Gavin, age 3

Hannah and Gavin, Christmas 2016

3.5 years old

Acknowledgments

I want to extend a heartfelt thank you to everyone who helped this book evolve from a simple idea to an actuality. First of all, I could never have completed this project without the help of my lifelong friends, Christina Pearson and Abbie Graham. Thank you both for your endless positivity about the book itself and also throughout our entire NICU journey. I can never thank you both enough for always believing in me and taking so much time out of your own busy lives to devote to editing this project. Who would have thought when we were in fifth grade English, working on our stories behind the cubbies, that we would still be editing together over twenty years later? A huge thank you to one of our wonderful NICU nurses, the same one who paused in the chaos that was delivery day to tell me congratulations, for editing and helping me sort through the endless medical information. You are an amazing person, and we love you! Thank you to Caroline Meek for becoming my publishing "coach;" your enthusiasm for writing and publication is an inspiration.

I would have to write another book to specifically list all of the people I need to acknowledge who cared for us and our children throughout our micropreemie journey. If you have read this book and you were part of our medical team, know that we appreciate each and every one of you and think of you all as family. Thank you to our neonatologists, neonatal nurse practitioners, nurses, respiratory therapists, social worker, occupational therapist, speech therapist, lactation consultants, nutritionists, and unit secretaries. Each of you has a gift. When work becomes busy or stressful, step back for a moment and let me represent all NICU parents when I say thank you. Thank you for saving my babies. Thank you for changing the world every day simply by going to work. Thank you to all of the volunteers who provided hats, blankets, toys and more during our four month stay. Every surprise you left made us smile and made the journey just a little bit easier.

Thank you to those of you who made our pregnancy possible from the very start. Thank you to our talented reproductive endocrinologist who began our miracle by believing it could be done and transforming four years of infertility into two very special babies. A special thanks to his wonderful nurse – without your constant support, I would never have made it through to IVF #4, which changed it all. We are also forever indebted to the most wonderful OB-GYN on the planet who was the first of many to save the lives of our twins. Thank you for understanding, thank you for being proactive and admitting me to the hospital, and thank you for being so kind to our family through it all. Without you, none of this would have been possible, and you will always hold a very special place in our hearts.

From the week we arrived home until the twins were three years old, we were so blessed to work with an amazing First Steps therapy team. You held my hand and guided me through the first three years, helping me as much as you helped the twins. I'll never forget how our children's faces lit up when they learned there would be therapy that day. You are some of our very favorite people in the world, and we will never forget everything you did for us. Thank you, Sherri, Suzanne, Amelia, Lori, and Denny. Thank you to Gavin's current therapy team – Beth, Jocelyn, and Scott. You each make therapy fun and challenging. It has been great watching him develop his "big kid" skills, and he has been so proud of his accomplishments – kicking, climbing, writing, cutting with scissors – and I thank each of you for believing in him.

Thank you to everyone I work with at Summit Rehab. Thank you for understanding my sudden departure during bedrest and my surprise move to part-time. You continue to be so flexible with me, understanding the need to put family first, and I am so grateful to work at such a wonderful place with such kind people. Thank you to Brian's coworkers and Burns and McDonnell for being so supportive during the twins' NICU stay. We love how this company places such an emphasis on the importance of family. Your dedication to your employees' well-being and happiness is amazing, and we are so grateful that Brian works at such an unbelievable company.

Thank you to all of our friends who kept us sane throughout our NICU journey. We sincerely appreciate all of the phone calls, texts, and hugs. A special thank you to Chris and Lori Yows and Eric and Stefanie Kratz for the amazing baby shower. Also, thank you so much to Amy Kuntz for your incredible photography. Thank you Tony and Alisa for sharing your story and giving us hope. To *all* of our friends – we love each of you so much and thank you for your visits, kindness, love and support. We are so grateful to have each of you in our lives.

Our family. Where to begin? We would not have made it through this without you, and words cannot ever express how much we appreciate you all. Thank you to my amazing parents, Dan and Donna Pearson, who never gave up and love our children more than I ever could have imagined possible. Thank you for thinking of them constantly, being at our house in an instant when we need you, and being the first ones to dive into tee-pees or spend hours coloring simply because two three-year-olds ask. Thank you to my wonderful in-laws Bill and Lee Evans, to my incredible Grandma and Grandpa Pearson, my sweet Grandma and Grandpa Hood, all of my amazing aunts, uncles, and cousins – our family is so lucky to have each and every one of you in our lives.

To Brian – thank you for your optimism and the way you can always make me laugh even when times are hard. Thank you for being the only person I can imagine who could have made me smile throughout four years of infertility and four months in intensive care. I loved you before our children, but after having seen you as a father – I love you more now than ever. Thank you for being my best friend through it all.

To Hannah and Gavin – thank you for how hard you fought to be here with us today. Thank you for never giving up when it was hard to breathe and when we continued to stick you with needles just to keep you alive. You have taught me that anything is possible if you have the courage to believe. Thank you for showing me what life is really about and for giving my life its purpose. You are my heroes, and I am forever grateful that I am your mom.

84938481R00115

Made in the USA
San Bernardino, CA
14 August 2018